ACHIEVEMENT OF DISTRICT PRIMARY EDUCATION PROGRAMME

ACHIEVEMENT OF DISTRICT PRIMARY EDUCATION PROGRAMME

By

Dr. Brundaban Chandra Mishra

Senior Lecturer in Education
D.P.I.A.S.E., Berhampur
District: Ganjam (Orissa)

&

Dr. Manoj Kumar Dash

Lecturer in Education
T.T. College, Purusottampur
District: Ganjam (Orissa)

SONALI PUBLICATIONS
NEW DELHI-110002

First Published-2005

ISBN 81-88836-73-7

Published by

SONALI PUBLICATIONS
4228/1, Ansari Road,
New Delhi-110 002 (India)
Phone: 23266109, 23279245 • Fax: 91-11-23253475

Printed at:

Amit Enterprises, Delhi

Preface

India stands committed to universalize elementary education ever since its constitution came into force in 1950. Universalisation of Elementary Education in India, a constitutional mandate, has been persistently pursued during the last five decades in the form of numerous State and Central programmes. With overriding emphasis initially laid on extension of provision of access, the Indian primary education system experienced a massive quantitative linear expansion emerging as a World's second largest network. Notwithstanding this impressive expansion during the post independence decades, the avowed goal of universalisation of primary education, let alone that U.E.E., continues to elude all efforts and initiatives. Our continued failure since independence to fulfil the constitutional directive of providing education to all children upto the age of 14 years is a teasing reality.

In fact, with National Policy on Education, 1986 (modified in 1992), delineating the three aspects of U.E.E. as, (i) Universal excess and enrolment, (ii) Universal retention of children until they attain the age of 14 years, and (iii) a substantial improvement in the learner achievement, the ask of achieving U.E.E. has become more daunting and challenging.

A few initiatives were launched in the past before the advent of the District Primary Education Programme (DPEP) to improve the 'quality and relevance' of primary education in the country. Significant among these are: (i) operation blackboard scheme, (ii) laying down minimum levels of learning; (iii) establishment of district institutes of education and training; (iv) decentralisation of educational planning and management. In the sense, all these initiatives were disjointed and fragmented efforts conceived in their own perspectives. They therefore, largely lacked linkage and a holistic operational framework. DPEP a "homegrown" programme, has been conceived, as a unique programme to help achieve the unfinished agenda of UEE. The DPEP intends to achieve UEE goals through developing and implementing a replicable, sustainable and cost-effective programme. With DPEP interventions and inputs put in place, it is expected that the existing state of primary education, from both supply and demand perspective, in DPEP districts would substantially improve.

The present volume reports the status of primary education in Orissa after DPEP intervention. The findings of the study are quite interesting. It is hoped that these findings will help the teachers, educational administrators and policy makers in more than one way.

The authors would like to appreciate the cooperation of the heads of the sample institutions, teachers and learners while collecting relevant data.

Special thanks are due to the U.G.C. authority for the financial support in conducting the present piece of work.

Dr. Brundaban Chandra Mishra

Dr. Manoj Kumar Dash

CONTENTS

1

INTRODUCTION

Primary education is the necessary foundation. Low educational achievement among certain population sections, particularly among the poor, scheduled castes, scheduled tribes and women is major constraint to their social and economic development.

Improvement in the standards of primary education depends largely on the augmented participation of those social strata, which had been difficult to reach or had eluded reach for some reason. There is a sense of urgency in the efforts of the Government to provided education to all children. Many programmes have been launched to accelerate the movement of Universalisation of primary education in our country.

DEVELOPMENT OF PRIMARY EDUCATION IN INDIAN CONTEXT

Before the establishment of British Empire, the old and traditional system of education was prevailed in the country. Britishers rule over a considerable long period in India. So the Indian system of Education since independence one of the most important question striking the attention of the Government was the question of providing basic Minimum Education for all children. The Education of the children of the country became the responsibility of the people of the country, India has been a land of learning throughout the ages, not in the sense that education has been universal, but learning has always been very highly valued. It is interesting to watch the pageant of Indian education move from ancient forest schools to the modern and fully equipped schools of today. "Education in India", as remarked by Howell, "Under the British Government was first ignored, then violently and successful opposed, then conducted in a system now universally admitted to be erroneous and finally placed on its present footing". Education development, has been deemed central to strengthening human resources for which of education has lost its key points and by the end of 18th century it become nonentity. After the battle of Plassey in 1759 some Indian education institutions made valiant efforts in the field of expansion of education. About one lakh primary schools were being run in Bengal itself. Despite of this tremendous efforts die ancient Indian education could not progress. Because the Britishers tried to stabilize their supremacy by modifying or overhauling the social, literacy and cultural values of the conquered country. Indian system of education is destroyed time to time under the influence of British education policy.

During the period of East India company up to 1857, no satisfactory steps was taken in the sphere of education. Soon after the revolt of 1857, the British parliament took over the administration of India. There period 1857 to 1887 were important in the history of primary education during pre-independent period. Because by 1882 nearly 29,000 primary schools with a capacity to teach 21 lakh students had been established in India. This measure was not adequate, because only 1.2% children could be made literate by this effort. Proper expansion of education. In India could not take place. The then Government took an unfortunate step of transferring the responsibility of primary education to local bodies which were found deficit. From 1882 to 1902, an increase of only 66 lakhs of students could be recorded at primary stage of education. But primary education expanded considerably during 1859 to 1881. During 1855 number of primary school was 2,810 and it become 82,916 in 1881-82.

Indian Education Commission (1882) made several recommendations for the expansion and improvement of primary education *i.e.*, responsibility, control and administration of primary education should be transferred to local bodies, the district boards or council in rural areas. Government resolution on Educational policy, 1904 declared that the Government of India fully accepted the proposition that the active extension of primary education was one of most important duties of the state.

1921 is a significant year in the history of primary education in India. In this year the control of primary education was transferred to Indian ministers. From 1921 onwards that the country accepted the goal of universal compulsory education and made efforts to realise it. In 1921-22, the number of primary school rose to 160,070 with an enrolment of 6.3 million. From 1921-1926, there was great spurt in the development of primary education. During this period number of primary school increased from 1,66,809 to 1,97,999 and their enrolment 6.96 million to 9.11 million.

Lord Curzon, the viceroy of India made commendable efforts for the expansion and development of primary education. He encouraged the Indian people in the sphere of education. After Lord Curzon primary education went into the hand of local bodies. Efforts were made to make primary education compulsory. In view of the utility of primary education, Maharaja Sayaji Rao Gaikward, the rulers of Baroda State, introduced compulsory primary education in some 52 villages of his state. An act was also passed in 1906 for the expansion of this scheme under which primary education was made compulsory for boys in the age group of 7 years to 12 years and for the girls in the age group of 7 years to 10 years.

Gopal Krishna Gokhale made speeches in the imperial legislative council in 1906, 1907 and 1908 suggesting that primary education be made free all over India and compulsory at some selected places. In 1910 he moved a resolution recommending "that a beginning be made in the direction of compulsory primary education throughout the country".

Vittal Bhai Patel introduced a Bill in the Provincial Legislative Assembly of Bombay to make primary education compulsory within the municipal limit of Bombay province. This bill become Act in 1918. The Act made its impact throughout the country and by 1930 primary education was made compulsory for the children between 6 to 10 years of age throughout India. A rapid expansion of primary education took place after the implementation of Primary Education Act. Unfortunately during the time of Hartog Committee slackness came in the speed of expansion of primary education.

"Introduction of Provincial Autonomy in 1937 removed the handicaps of the expansion of primary education. Each Province, prepared programmes for the expansion and improvement of primary education. Establishment of primary schools in rural areas was emphasized. As a result compulsory education become available for children of 10,017 rural areas and 229 towns by 1947. Besides, arrangement of primary education for girls was made in 1404 villages and 10 towns.

CONSTITUTIONAL PROVISION

Our constitution made it a Directive Principle of the state policy, "to provide free and compulsory education for all children up to the age of fourteen years within ten years from the date on which the constitution come in to force." Education is a means to achieve the ideals and values enshrined in the constitution. So the constitution of India has made provisions under a number of Articles and clauses for education.

In 1976, the 42nd Amendment of the constitution included education in the concurrent list which provided scope for the union Government for higher share and better participation, in the sphere of education.

Article 41 promises the right to education. It states "The State shall within the limits of its economic capacity, make effective provisions for securing right to work, to education".

Article 45 relates to the provision of free and compulsory education. "The state shall endeavour to provide, within a period of 10 years from the commencement of this constitution, for free and compulsory education for all children until they complete the age 14 years".

Article 46 relates to educational and economic interest of SC, ST and other weaker sections. "The state shall promote with special care the educational and economic interests of the weaker sections of the people and in particular the SC and ST and shall protect them from social injustice and all forms of exploitation".

Article 350 relates to facilities for instruction in mother tongue at primary stage. It shall endeavour of every state and every local authorities within the state to provide adequate facilities for instruction in the mother tongue at primary stage of education to children belonging to Linguistic minority group and the President may issue any direction to any state as he considers necessary, for proper security to the provision of such facilities.

Article 15 states that the state shall not discriminate any citizen on the grounds only of sex.

UNIVERSALISATION OF PRIMARY EDUCATION

Elementary education is fundamental to the eradication of poverty, fostering economic progress, managing the growth of population and creating a clean and healthy environment. There can not be effective empowerment of Indians without universal primary education. Again there can not be UEE without the full participation of the girl child and the marginal and disadvantaged groups. Ever since Independence, India has been striving to universalise elementary education, which is a constitutional obligation. The endeavours to universalise received a fillip from the National Policy of Education (NPE), 1986 which strongly articulated the equity and empowerment dimensions of education. World wide Universalisation of Elementary Education (UEE) is increasingly perceived as a civil right indispensable for human development, be it socio-economic development, poverty irradiation, democratic practice or good governance. Equity in education is the inevitable prelude to social equity at large. Education is perceived to be an agent of basic change in the status of women and playing a positive, intervention rule in the empowerment of women to neutralise the accumulated distortions of the past.

CONCEPT OF UEE

In India UEE means making education available to all children in age group 6 to 14 years and in classes I to VIII.

Opportunity for this education may be provided through formal and Non-formal means of education. It signifies that education is for all and not for a selected few. This concepts accepts that education is the birth right of every child *i.e.,* all children belonging to rich and poor, living in towns as well as rural areas and in places which are accessible with difficulty have to be provided facilities for elementary education. Universalisation of education implies the followings:

1. Universalisation of Provision

It implies that adequate schooling must be provided to all children between age group 6 to 14 years in the country. It means primary schools are to be set up within 1 Km from the habitation of the child. It aims at bringing every home and every village on the educational map.

2. Universal Enrolment

Second phase is to see how to enroll all students in primary schools who attain the age 6 years *i.e.,* educable age. Government have made provision to enroll all children between age 6-14 years in primary schools.

3. Universalisation of Retention

It is the third phase of the UEE. Steps should be taken by which the enrolment of children must remain in school till the completion of primary education, *i.e.,* completion of school study, in primary education, the main objective is the attainment of stable literacy through a minimum of five year schooling. After entering the school if he/she leaves it or withdrawn from the school before completion, it leads to wastage in education, which create another problem.

4. Universal Participation

For the success of UEE, participation of community is quite inevitable. Community must be mobilised to take responsibility for the identification of needs, to take decisive role in ensuring the implementation of the programme of UEE. It require decentralization of educational administration.

5. Universalisation of Achievement

For the success of UEE, achievement of learner is to be ascertained. The strategy is to lay down learning outcomes expected from learners at elementary stage. The outcome is to be based on minimum level of learning (MLL) which is common to both formal-Non-formal programmes.

IMPORTANCE OF UEE

Naik, (1975) aptly observed: "The progress of primary education is an index of general, social and economic development of a country as a whole". Primary education plays an important rule in laying the proper foundation of a child's cultural, emotional, intellectual, moral, physical, social and spiritual development. Primary education contribute to the national development too. Various studies have clearly demonstrated that countries which have made proper provision of primary education are far ahead than those with inadequate provision.

Education is essential, for improving productivity and for bringing about desirable changes for social as well as national development. In 1946, the international community charged UNESCO with the responsibility for promoting education throughout the world due to its vital importance to individual and social well being. In 1948, the united nations in Paris proclaimed universal declaration of Human Right including the Right to Education. Article 26 states "Everyone has the right to education. Education shall be free at least in the elementary and fundamental stages". Hence elementary education shall be compulsory. India being the largest democracy of the world has the greatest stigma and darkest blemish of having the half of the world's illiterates. The UEE has been adopted as a national goal and Education for All (EFA) has been regarded as the international goal for promoting national well being, individual excellence and success of democracy.

PRESENT POSITION OF UEE

Article 45 of the constitution of India directed states to endeavour to provide within a period of 10 years of the commencement of die constitution free and compulsory education to all children up to the age of 14 years. This resolve to be fulfilled by 1960 was however. Severely hampered by several problems, such the in flux of displaced persons after partition and scarcity of resources, both financial and human.

As a result, the target date had to be first revised to 1970, then to 1976 and later to 1990. The target date according to NPE, 1986 is 1995. The modified policy, 1992 has further revised the target date. It states "It shall be ensure that free and compulsory education of satisfactory quality is provided to all children up to 14 years of age before we enter the 21st century. A national mission will be launched for the achievement of this goal".

The gross enrolment during 1950-51 was 42.6 per cent. It increased to 101.03 during 1990-91, At the middle stage this increased from 2.6 per cent to 60.11 per cent.

Enrolment at the primary stage increased about five fold from 19.2 million to 108.2 million in 1993-94. An analysis of the data revels that the population of children moving up from the primary to upper primary stage has been increasing steadily, from 16.3 per cent in 1950-51 to 42.5 per cent in 1993-94. The gross enrolment ratio of children in the age group 6-11 years increased from 42.6 per cent in 1950-51 to 101.5 per cent during 1990-1991 and 104.5 per cent during 1993-94. Likewise, the gross enrolment of 1-14 years age group increased from 12.7 per cent in 1950-51 to 67.7 per cent in 1993-94.

India has made great strides towards the goal of UEE since 1947. There has been significant progress in terms of spread of institutions, participation and equalisation of educational opportunities. The literacy rate has nearly trebled since independence. Access to schooling has been substantially achieved at the primary stage with 95 per cent of the rural population having access to primary school within one Kilo-Meter radius. The number of primary and upper primary school in the country has gone up from 223 thousands in 1950-51 to 728 thousands in 1993-94.

There is a strong regional dimension to UEE. Though the gross enrolment ratio at primary stage in India as a whole and in most of the states exceeds 100 per cent, still there are quite a few states. Where the ratio is considerably lower. These include Utter Pradesh, Bihar, Rajasthan, Haryana, Jammu and Kashmir and Meghalaya. At upper primary stage these states and, in addition, Andhra Pradesh, Orissa and Sikkim have GER's lower than the national average. The literacy rate of most of these states are also lower than the national average. The problem gets more completed as the dropout rates, though declining. Continue to be high. Regional disparities abound in rates of the drop-outs also.

Gender disparities are conspicuous in regard to enrolment and retention. Girls enrolment has grown at the primary stage from 5.4 million in 1950-51 to 46.4 million in 1993-94 and at the upper primary stage from 0.5 million to 15.7 million. Rate of growth of enrolment of girls has been higher than that of boys but disparities still persists. Girls still account for only 42.88 per cent of the enrolment at the primary stage and 39.34 per cent at upper primary stage. The droop-out rates of girls at the primary as well as the upper primary stage are higher than those of boys.

Another dimension of UEE is the participation in the educational process by the scheduled castes and scheduled tribes. Because of the affirmative policies of the Government, the enrolment of SCs and STs has increased considerably at primary stage. The participation of SCs and STs is more or less in proportion to their share in population at primary level.

Though concerted efforts are being made by the central and state Governments, UEE is still in the distant horizon. Recent studies on the trend of enrolment indicates that going by past trends UEE is likely to be achieved by 2006. It is the upper primary stage that more efforts are needed, as the gross enrolment needed to achieve universal participation in primary education (I-V) is likely to be achieved by 2001. The past can not and should not necessarily be the guide for the future. Nation as a whole should put in the extra efforts needed to accelerates the trends. So that we can ensure free and compulsory education to satisfactory quality to all children up to 14 years of age before we enter the 21st century, as envisaged in the NPE, 1986.

PROBLEMS OF UEE

Discussions, seminars and other workshops conducted by different agencies, at different accessions and surveys undertaken by Government and Non-Government agencies reached at the conclusion that there are several factors responsible for slow progress in the primary education among minorities.

- Low priority to primary education.
- Inadequate educational opportunities.
- Low enrolment of the backward section of the society.
- Stagnation.
- Wastage.
- Low enrolment of girls.
- Apathy the proverty of the parents.
- Defective curriculum.
- Uninspiring methods of teaching.
- Lack of suitable reading and writing material for children.
- Lack of qualified teachers.
- Frequent transfer of teachers.
- Lack of effective inspection and academic guidance by the inspecting staff.
- Failure to enforce compulsory attendance.
- Lack of a suitable admission policy.
- Conservative attitude towards co-education.
- Inadequate and unattractive school building.
- Poor nutrition of children.
- Existence of large number of incomplete primary schools.
- Lack of part-time facilities.
- Group rivalries of local bodies.

- Meagre financial out lays.
- Over population.
- Inadequate educational institutions in tribal areas.
- Problems of getting men and women teachers from the tribal group.
- Problems of medium of instruction.
- Problems of examination of evaluation.
- Delinking the education with life situation.
- Lack of motivation.
- Inadequate text books.

RESPONSE TO THE CHALLENGE

Primary education should be developed on priority basis and percentage of budget under this area should be increased suitably. There has been a decline in this sector. From 56 per cent of the total educational budget spent on primary education during the first five year plan. It come down .gradually in successive plans.

Though efforts are taken to improve the status of elementary education, in reality, the child in an actual classroom is not focussed fully and properly. Unless the child is focussed as the centre of the classroom activity, dropouts and stagnation will be the outcome.

PROGRAMME TO THE CHALLENGE

There are both qualitative and quantitative lacunae in the way of making primary education universal, free and compulsory. Expansion of primary education being the need of the hour, the ideal standard of quality that we try to fix may not be maintained. Attempt should be taken to tide the ground of population and again concrete steps with all devotion, missionary zeal enthusiasm both at public and Government level will enable us to reach the goal. Different agencies of UNO have been extending helping hands to realise the goal of UEE.

Since independence the government of India have been emphasizing on it. All measures to meet the essential requisites of UEE one being taken, to reach the national goal.

EDUCATIONAL POLICY

India has taken significant policy decisions to meet the many challenges in the field of education. Education was brought in to the list of concurrent subject by he 42nd amendment of the constitution in 1976 to facilitate evaluation of all India policies. The NPE 1986 envisaged concurrency as a "meaningful Partnership between the centre and state". NPF, and the Programme of Action, 1992 resolve to fulfil the constitution mandate of providing free and compulsory education of satisfactory quality to all children up to 14 years of age before the advent of the 21st century. The NPE introduced some new approaches far the achievement UEE these includes :

(1) A shift from the state to the districts as the unit of planning.

(2) A stress upon social mobilization to promote literacy.

(3) Non-formal Education Programmes as a strategy to provide education to dropouts and out of school children.

The NPE gave priority to :

- Expansion of early childhood care and Education (ECCE),
- Universalisation of Elementary Education (UEE),
- Non-formal, adult and continuing education.

The above facts includes access to and participation in elementary education far all children up to the age of 14 years and achievement of at least minimum level of learning;

- Creation of necessary structure, and the setting in motion of processes which could empower women make education an instrument of women's equality.
- Improvement of the content and process of education to related better to the environment, people's culture, their leaving and working conditions.

- A shift in the emphasis from enrolment preset to enrolment as well as retention and achievement.

The essential commitment of the NPE 1986. Towards achieving UEE was reiterated at the E-9 summit for EFA at New Delhi in 1993. An important land mark at the summit was the announcement that 6 per cent of the GDP would be spent on education.

REVISED NPE/POA, 1992

For UEE an increasing importance to Minimum Level of Learning (MLL) along with access and retention of children.

- Scope of operation Blackboard will be enlarged to provide minimum pucca rooms and three teachers in every Primary School. Facilities will be provided to upper primary schools.
- Revised policy 1992 envisage that free and compulsory education of satisfactory quality will be provided to all children up to 14 years before 21st century.
- A annual mission will be campaigned to achieve UEE by the AD 2000.
- A new scheme of voluntary school system will be launched to fulfil the needs and requirements of neglected, hilly tribals and inaccessible areas where no schooling facilities are available.
- Central Government well gender financial assistance to voluntary schools.
- To facilitation large enrolment and retention of girls, at least 50 per cent of teachers appointed will be ladies.
- "Steps will be taken to lesson the load of school bag on little children.

The first step of making education compulsory is to prepare the ground for the same by passing an Act of parliament and notified it in the official gazette. Rules, as per specifications, are to be prepared and also passed by both houses of parliament.

ACTION TO MAKE PRIMARY EDUCATION COMPULSORY

Preparation of a scheme, by the specified authority to make education compulsory in an area.

- Obtaining Government approval for the scheme.
- Notification of a scheme of compulsion within the specified area.
- Appointment of attendance officers.
- Preparation of lists of children under compulsion and sending notices to parents whose children are now of school going age.
- Ascertain attendance status of child.
- Taking action against parents of non-attending children.

The enforcement of compulsion, compels the educational authorities to take note of each and every child resident in an area, provide him/her with suitable educational facilities, even for part time education; If need be and monitor the attendance of every child, and fellow up all cases of non-attendance.

As in management of traffic, very seldom need penal provisions be invoked, but there is a need to get the massage across that children have a right to education and the state is there to ensure that children are able to avail of that right. And of course, the state too, should be there visibly and assertively to protect its children. As in other areas of education, the DPEP districts may be expected to show others the way. The DPEP districts, with the help of the programme should all soon be ready in terms of the facilities available and the quality of education they to offer.

The District Primary Education programme reflects the current concerns stated in the NPE as well as the constitutional commitment of Article 45 for ensuring free and compulsory education to all children up to the age of fourteen.

The legislative support system, called compulsory education laws have been in force in many states in India since 1920s. Purpose of these "to legislation's is to provide for free and compulsory primary education", these legislation's, do not in fact, by themselves make education 'compulsory', but only 'enable' the 'local authorities' to do so. The compulsory education Acts in India today, are therefore, merely 'enabling legislation's'.

Provisions exist within all DPEP states to respond to the all of Article 45 of the constitution to make education compulsory, but the more passing of compulsory education acts do not make education compulsory in state. It may be argued that Article 45 merely asked the state to "endeavour to provide" provision no doubt, has been attempted take primary education to all, but what the constitution was not just a stage of education but also a methodology for ensuring the right to primary education. Provision of educational facilities, perhaps only an opportunity, perhaps even a right on that facility, but 'Compulsory Education' was a method of protecting children's right to education when the parents through neglect or ignorance pay no attention to this need.

STRATEGY TO REDUCE DROPOUT

- Creation of parental awareness.
- Mobilization of community.
- Utilization of institutional mechanism created through the 73rd and 74th constitutional Amendments.
- Provision of economic incentives to help poor families defray the cost of education.
- Convergence of services in the areas of ICDS, primary education, primary health and creches.
- Recognizing the content and process of education.
- Improving the quality.
- Making learning child centered.
- Making school environment attractive.
- Motivation of teacher.
- Training of teacher.
- Implementation of new district primary education programme initiative, which is essentially targeted towards low female literacy.

NEW APPROACH TO ELEMENTARY EDUCATION

In the policy of the Government of India as outlined in NPE, 1986 and EFA declaration, certain new approaches were adopted by the Government of India. These addressed diverse issues like learning, achievement, community involvement and local specificity.

Reorganizing the need to provide all children with access to education of comparable standard, the NPE 1986, recommended lying down of MLL for primary classes in subject such as language, mathematics and environmental studies. These apply both to formal as well as non-formal streams and consider the realistic, relevant and functional aspect of learning.

The MLL approach seeks to focus on a minimum quantum of learning which practically all children, even disadvantaged, can acquire. The effort is therefore, to combine quality with equity. Achievement is defined in terms of acquisition of competencies. Every child is expected to master the basic minimum competencies by the end of the corresponding age or stage of development. Competency is different from the traditional memorization of content or completion of syllabus.

Teaching is directed towards ensuring that all children master the basic competencies by end of primary level. The approach of MLL envisages definite changes in the teaching learning process by making them

- competency-based
- activity oriented
- interesting

This approach has become an integral part of programmes of DPEP. The issue of content vs. concept, understanding vs. role memorization and unachievable load vs. achievable set of competencies have been addressed in MLL approach.

Community participation and community ownership of an educational programme is highly indexed for its success. Therefore, community mobilisation to manage, implement and monitor the educational facilities at the village level is being pursued. All educational interventions are designed according to the need of the community, accountable to and monitored by the-community.

The 73rd and 74th Amendment Art, 1992 (Panchyat Raj Act) provided for democratically elected bodies at the district, sub-district, Panchyat and municipal level to deal with educational, health and other development programme within their jurisdiction. Village education committees are being constituted for this proposes. This is a positive step in the direction of micro planning and decentralization. Micro planning implies area specific planning where, the unit might be a village, block or district. Decentralization connotes the possibility of adjusting school calendar/timing to suit the local socio-economic conditions. Hence community mobilisation, micro planning and decentralization must exist concurrently in order to be most effective.

PROGRAMMES FOR UEE

The commitment to achieve UEE have leads to several successful strategies and programmes being undertaken.

(i) Non-Formal Education (NFE)

It was started in 1976. It can reach out to children not covered by the formal education system. It is designed to offer learning opportunities to children in age 6-14 years who, because of certain socio-economic factors, have remained outside the fold of the formal education system.

(ii) Operation Black-Board (OB)

It was launched in 1987 to provide the minimum essential infrastructure in the primary schools. The inputs included two teachers in all primary schools, essential teaching, learning material and at least two classrooms in an all-weather building. The scheme is now being expanded to upper primary schools. It is aimed that OB schools will be provided with three teachers.

(iii) National Literacy Mission (NLM)

It was set up by central Government in 1988 for the eradication of illiteracy in the age group 15-35 years age group.

Although the main focus of the total literacy campaigns (TLCS) undertaken with the NLM is to cover the entire adult population in an area specific time bound, volunteer based, cost effective and also outcome oriented mode, literacy classes for children in the age group 6-14 years are held simultaneously, wherever possible.

(iv) District Primary Education Programme (DPEP)

It is the most ambitious primary education programme so far. Launched in 1994 in 42 districts in 7 states. Today it covers 153 states of more than 219 districts.

DPEP builds upon accumulated national experience in pursuit of UEE as well as experience gained from state-specific and area-specific project such as Andhra Pradesh primary education programme (APPEP), Bihar education project (BEP), Utter Pradesh basic education project (UPBEP), and Lok Jumbish. DPEP is a home grown, district specific programme emphasizing access, retention and of quality of learning.

CONCEPT OF DPEP

In a vast country such as India, with a number of languages of instruction, education has to be contextual. Contextually entails local area-planning with disaggregated targets and decentralized planning and management. The district plans are prepared through an intensive process of interaction with the local bodies, teachers and NGOs so that they are "owned" by all who are to be associated in its implementation and thus reflecting the ground level realities. It ensures that development planning is more responsive and adaptable to regional and local needs of the people. These bodies have an important role to play in the reconstruction of educational system. DPEP envisages the micro-planning will be the focus of the programme.

DPEP has been designed to improve quality of teaching and learning; increase retention and expand access. The areas of pedagogical intervention are:

1. Development of curriculum, textbook and materials.
2. Teacher training with an emphasis on multi-grade and activity based teaching.

3. Institution building at various levels to extend training and academic support.
4. Decentralisation of academic resources.
5. Actualization of support structure at block and cluster level.
6. Setting up of block resource centre for peer interaction decentralized training and academic supervision and support.
7. Strengthening the existing structures and resource institutions.
8. Capacity building for teachers. Government functionaries, and officials as well as community leaders.

DPEP is based on the principle of additionality and provides for additional school building, classroom teachers, other materials and infrastructural support as and when needed, ensuring convergence of various services and networking available resource all around.

BACKGROUND OF DPEP

National Policy of Education, 1986 (as updated in 1992) and the programme of Action, 1992 (POA) reaffirm the national commitment to Universalisation of Elementary Education (UEE), para 5.12 of NPE resolves that free and compulsory education of satisfactory quality should be provided to all children up to 14 years of age before we enter 21st century. The NPE also specifies in para 5.5 that UEE has three aspects;

1. Universal access and Enrolment.
2. Universal retention of children up to 14 years of age.
3. A substantial improvement in quality of education to enable all children to achieve essential level of learning.

Right from independence India has preserved the goal of UEE, even though substantial progress has been achieved, the goal still remains elusive. The additional participation in elementary education has to come from social strata and regions which are more difficult to reach.

Therefore, the path that lies ahead in the march to UEE is more arduous. It requires higher intensity of effort and more systematic planning and implementation.

National experience with the pursuit of UEE had established the following;

1. The contextuality various widely across the country. Much requires to be done in respect of quality and achievement. Hence pursuit of UEE would be mainly in the area of quality, facilities, achievement, participation and demand aspects etc. needs more attention.

2. Planning for UEE had hitherto been mainly at the national and state level. Planning should be from below, right from the village upwards, but given the objective conditions, a beginning has to be made with the district as the unit of planning.

   Plans are to be prepared through the process of integration's, with the help of local bodies, teachers and NGOs, so as to reflect the ground level realities.

3. Financial and non-financial side need to complement higher allocation of resources.

4. Emphasis should be given on access in terms of construction of classrooms and appointment of teachers needs to be augmented by :

   a. A holistic planning and management approach, to perceives the task of UEE in its totality integrates all the measures need to achieve UEE.

   b. All aspects of planning and implementation should incorporate a gender perspective. It should be an integral part of all measures needed to achieve UEE.

   c. Access to girls, disadvantaged group and out of school children is more difficult aspect in the way to achieve UEE.

   d. Improving effectiveness of the school.

e. Strengthening alternatives to schooling *i.e.*, non-formal education system.

f. Stressing the process of participation where local community facilitates participation, achievement and school effectiveness.

g. Tuning up the competence, training and motivation of teachers.

h. Stressing learning competence and achievement.

i. Stressing need for improved teaching/learning materials.

j. Accelerating the process of planning and management in respect of both existing and creative areas.

k. Convergence between elementary education and related services.

5. The DPEP also build upon the experience gained in:

   a. The implementation of the Bihar Education Project (with UNICEF assistance) and Lok Jumbish Project (with SIDA assistance).

   b. The planning of basic education project in Uttar Pradesh (with ID assistance).

   c. The implementation of the Andhra Pradesh primary education project with (ODA assistance), Shiksha Karmi Project (with SIDA assistance) and Mahila Samakhya (with DUTCH) assistance.

In BEP and UP project too, investment is concentrated in the chosen districts and district specific investment is completed by a few state level interventions such as strengthening of state level institutions. Where the project goes beyond the Uttar Pradesh and Bihar Projects, is in

1. The emphasis of local area planning with the district plans being formulated in their own right rather than being derived from a state plan project document.

2. Greater rigour and infusion of professional inputs in planning and appraisal.
3. Focussed targeting in the district selected would be; Educationally backward districts with female literacy below the national average and districts where TLCs have been successful leading to enhanced demand for elementary education.
4. More focussed coverage is that the DPEP would focus on primary stage (classes I-V and its NFE equivalent), with stress on education for girls, and for socially disadvantaged groups. In states where enrolment and retention is near universal in the primary stage, support can be considered for the upper primary stage.
5. The objective of DPEP is to gradually extend the coverage to all the districts which satisfy one of the twin criteria referred to in para 1.5(iii). The pace of expansion would depend upon the availability of resources and in states where the programme is now being started on the pace and quality of implementation in die selected districts.
6. The DPEP would develop and implement in the districts selected a replicable, sustainable and cost effective programme :
   (i) To reduce difference in enrolment, dropout and learning achievement among gender and social groups to less than five per cent.
   (ii) To reduce overall primary dropout rates for all students to less than ten per cent.
   (iii) To raise average achievement level by at least, twenty five per cent over measured base line level.
   (iv) To ensure achievement of basic literacy and numeracy competencies and a minimum of forty per cent achievement level in other competencies, by all primary school children.
   (v) To provide, according to national norms, access for all children, to primary classes (I-V) *i.e.*, primary

schooling whenever possible, or its equivalent non-formal education.

The DPEP would also strength the capacity of national, state and districts institutions and organizations for the planning, management and evaluation of primary education.

8. The DPEP is being implemented in a mission mode through registered state level autonomous societies. Each society has two organs.

   1. A general council with chief minister as ex-officer president and
   2. Executive committee under the chairmanship of chief secretary/education secretary of the state.

   The executive responsibility vests with the state programme Director being member secretary of the executive committee and the council. Government of India would represent in the General council and the executive committee. The plan would be formulated and implemented with the active association with the community, NGOs, teachers and educationists. Therefore all these group would have to be provided adequate representation and vice the management of the DPEP project at all levels; state, district, block and village.

9. The district plans would be rigorously appraised and their implementations are systematically monitored.

10. Fund would be released from Govt. of India to the state level societies. GOI contribution is expected to be of the order of eighty five per cent and is likely to follow the existing pattern for release to IDA projects.

11. DPEP is not a finance driven programme but seeks to build systems that are cost effective, replicable and sustainable. The construction component would be limited to twenty four per cent and management cost to six per cent. The recurring liabilities at the end of the programme would be the exclusive responsibility of the state Government.

Appraisal would be with respect to the criteria of equity, participative processes, feasibility, sustainability and replicability.

DEVELOPMENT OF DISTRICT PRIMARY EDUCATION PROGRAMME

The 1990s is marked as a real breakthrough in attitudes and perceptions in education. It is realised that the unreached can not be reached with more of the same. Hence, radical alternatives are being pioneered. India plans to increase the spending on primary education. Though there are major challenges ahead, Universalisation is a feasible task, given the political commitment of central and State Governments, the enhanced allocation are bring provided to elementary education, the new ambience created by the Panchayati Raj Legislation, the total literacy campaigns and new initiative like the District Primary Education Programme.

By the use of conventional as well as unconventional methods. India is progressing towards the goal of education for all, with the awareness that success in educating its population will mean redeeming a pledge long-unfulfilled.

In the beginning of 21st century it is now universally accepted that effective policies should be put in place tc protect public expenditure on primary education, as an integral part of national development country like India yet to universalize basic education. Naturally basic education is entitled to a high priority in public expenditure success of literacy campaigns in many part of the country with their emphasis on : (i) Area-specific planning, (ii) social mobilisation and (iii) innovative use of media and communication, paved the way of District Primary Education Programme (DPEP). The basic premise of the DPEP is to Universalisation is on textual and can be achieved only if the issues of quantity, quality and management are simultaneously addressed. It is developed on Indian experienced with the pursuit of universal primary education. It is an experiment in the use of the project made for the implementation of policy. It is targeted on low female literacy districts, it adopts the project mode to hasten the Universalisation in selected districts, it seeks to transgress the limitations of the project mode. It seeks to be a beachhead for transforming the entire system and mechanisms are being put in place for evaluating the innovations in the project and incorporate them into the rest of the system wherever felt desirable.

DPEP is a major initiative to achieve UEE. It adopts a holistic view of primary education and seeks to operationalise the strategy of UEE through district specific planning and disaggregated target setting. It has emerged as the important vehicle for UEE as well as for international assistance. A National Elementary Education Mission has been established in August 1995 with DPEP as its core. The macro objectives of the mission would be to bring to bear upon the UEE a sense of expedition and resolve and to take concerted action in partnership with states, local bodies, teachers and NGOs towards UEE.

DPEP guidelines were formulated in April 1993. In December 1993 the cabinet accorded its approval for the scheme in principle. In 1994, January planning commission approved DPEP as a centrally sponsored scheme. Project districts were selected in 42 districts spread over seven states. Assam, Haryana, Madhya Pradesh, Karnataka, Maharashatra, Tamilnadu and Kerala. DPEP planning processes have provided a valuable opportunity for NCERT/NIEPA to field test many of the pedagogical and management concepts that they have been developing over the years. Studies conducted to identity area—specific interventions in each of the districts. In May 1994 finance committee of the Government of India has approved details of the DPEP proposals and its financial parameters.

Again a three day programme for planning and designing of Baseline Assessment study proposals for the state Himachal Pradesh, Orissa and Gujarat was organised by NCERT from September 21-23, 1995 in New Delhi. Its main objective is directed to project a true picture of the primary schools. Which would identify the weakest link which determines the strength of the chain.... DPEP was extended to selected districts of Andhara Pradesh and West Bengal in 1994-95.

BASIC OBJECTIVES OF DPEP

DPEP was launched in the year 1994 with twin purposes *i.e.,*

1. Operationalise decentralized planning and management.
2. To accelerate the pace of UPE in the country.

Consciously the districts, wherein the female literacy was lower than the national average and where the total literacy campaign has generated enough demand for UEE were selected for implementation of the programme. DPEP which emphasizes on contextuality, aims at reducing gender and social disparities that do prevail in existing system. More specially DPEP aims at fulfilling the objectives:

- to reduce difference in enrolment dropout and leaning achievement among gender and social groups :
- to reduce overall primary dropout rate for all students.
- to raise average achievement level.
- to ensure achievement of basic literacy and numeracy competencies.
- to provide according to national norms access for all children to primary education classes (I-V).

MODE OF FULFILLING THE BASIC OBJECTIVES:

The above objectives can be fulfilled by taking into consideration of the following steps :

- improving school practice through the use of information systems;
- improving school practice through decentralizing information about the education system;
- improving school practice through community participation;
- improving school practice through curriculum development;
- improving school practice through preservice teacher education;

- improving school practice through revision of text books;
- improving school practice through multigrade classrooms;
- improving school practice through the use of National testing.

STATUS OF DPEP

The DPEP programme was formally launched on November 8, 1994. Well into its eighth year of implementation. The DPEP amply testifies to the nature and intensity of the planning process, the integration of professional inputs, participative planning and management, and the emphasis on capacity building that have gone into the entire process. Since 1994 the tasks of putting up the systems and setting the process in motion has gathered momentum. Computerised management information system at national level has been set up. National management structures for DPEP have been notified (the general council and the project board). Technical support group is strengthened to assist DPEP planning and implementation has made functional, annual work plans of states and national component appraised and approved, fund flow systems established, statewise gender and tribal interventions developed, quarterly supervision of states undertaken and needs assessment in capacity building has been done.

The project board is an empowered body assigned with full financial and administrative powers to implement the programme. It would recommend the policies, consider. Annual Work Plans and Budget (AWPBS), approve norms for new programme components and activities promote convergence guidance to the Bureau.

NATIONAL MANAGEMENT STRUCTURE (NMS)

The NMS for DPEP at apex level comprises of a General Council (GS), a Project Board (PB), a DPEP Bureau with concomitant staff and the consultancy arrangements with Ed. CIL for technical support to the programme. General council is presided over by the Union Minister for Human Resource

Development, it would provide policy direction to the DPEP and facilitate centre-state co-ordination. The project board is an empowered body assigned with full financial and administrative powers to implement the programme. It would recommend the policies, consider Annual Work Plans and Budget (AWPBs), approve norms for new programme components and activities, promote convergence of services, review DPEP progress and provide guidance to the Bureau. It is headed by the education secretary and has representatives not below the rank of joint secretary of the concern departments and the financial advisor. The joint secretary of DPEP Bureau is the Member Secretary of the project board. It would meet at least once every quarter and more frequently if needed.

DPEP Bureau is assisted by the Ed. CIL Technical support group (TSG) a core group, of technical and professional experts on contract, supplemented as needed by short term consultants, to provide Key technical services for the programme. This has provided a high degree of flexibility and accessing professional competence for the programme.

The thrust areas of activity of the planning unit of the TSG are focus on training on the various facets of planning including project planning, micro planning, planning for gender and disadvantaged groups, training module development, and capacity building assistance for project planning in states implementing DPEP.

STATE MANAGEMENT STRUCTURE (SMS)

Administrative arrangements have been set up in all states and DPEP districts for implementation of the programme. Autonomous societies as nodal bodies for project implementation has been registered and fully activated in all the states they represent a joint partnership between GOI and the state governments for project implementations. The design of the DPEP societies provides for GOI representation both in general council and Executive committee. Nominees are both official and non-officials. All GOI nominees are educationists, person working on SC/ST education's, experts on women education and person from Non Government sectors.

Administrative, service and financial regulations have been adopted in all societies for basic operational procedures, and they lay down financial delegations fund flows, recruitment procedures, norms for travel, workshops, meetings, service matters etc.

A process of continuous dialogue and interaction between GOI and state project officers (SPOs) have been set in motion and is ensured through a variety of modes.

A monthly Demi-official letter from the state education secretaries to the joint secretary, DPEP Bureau, concerning progress, problems if any, technical support if needed have been systematized. Quarterly MIS report, quarterly EC meetings and annual GC meetings other modalities.

States implementing comprehensive basic education projects would gradually be reinforced through rigorous training for planning and community mobilization.

The nature of EC decision making for programme implementation in the basic ground of the DPEP has been ensured. The decisions includes :

1. Creation of post for project management.
2. Adoption of service.
3. Financial regulations.
4. Approving pattern for new institutional structures.
5. Contractual arrangement for professional assistance.

A process of continuous dialogue and interaction between GOI and state project officers (SPOs) have been set in motion and is ensured through a variety of modes.

2

CONTEXT OF THE STUDY

RATIONALE OF THE STUDY

Primary education plays a pivotal role in the lives of people as it lays the foundation of learning and equips them with basic skills for their survival both as individuals and as the members of society. Universalisation of Elementary Education (UEE) has, therefore, assumed great significance and all out efforts are being made accordingly by the government and by voluntary organizations to achieve it. A few initiatives were launched in the past before the advent of the District Primary Education Programme (DPEP) to improve the quality and relevance of primary education in the country. Significant among these are:

(i) operation blackboard scheme;

(ii) laying down minimum levels of learning;

(iii) establishment of District Institutes of Education and training; and

(iv) decentralisation of educational planning and management. In a sense, all these initiatives were disjointed and piecemeal efforts representing system level reform initiatives. DPEP, a "homegrown" progra-mme, has been conceived, as a unique programme to help achieve the unfinished agenda of UEE. In reality, DPEP seeks to operationalise (vide para 7.4.6) the POA, 1992 which reads as follows:

Further efforts would be made to develop district specific projects, defined responsibilities, definite time-schedule and specific targets; each district project will be prepared with the major strategy framework and will be tailored to the specific needs and possibilities in the district. Apart from effective UEE, the goal of each project will include the reduction of existing disparities in educational access, the provision of alternative systems of comparable standards to the disadvantaged groups, a substantial improvement in the quality of schooling facilities, obtained a genuine community involvement in the running schools, and building up local level capacity to ensure effective decentralisation of educational planning. That is to say, the overall goal of the project would be reconstruction of primary education as a whole in selected districts instead of a piecemeal implementation of schemes. An integrated approach is more likely to achieve synergies among different programme components.

Ayyer (1993) briefly highlighted the key elements of the DPEP as local planning with community participation; a holistic approach, a 'matrix' of networking between district, state and national institutions as well as between educational, management and social science institutions; an emphasis on capacity building; rigorous professional input and a focus on girls and other socially disadvantaged groups.

The DPEP intends to achieve UPE goals through developing and implementing a replicable, sustainable and cost-effective programme (DPEP Guidelines, 1997) are:

The DPEP interventions and strategies are based on the contextual realities and community - specific needs and aspirations, identified through open and democratic consultative processes with the people. They have emerged from: (i) a consistent and reliable database; (ii) Findings of research studies conducted specifically for the programme; and (iii) intense consultative processes. The DPEP interventions and strategies have been designed to address the issues and problems that besiege the Indian primary education system. DPEP interventions include: (i) Community mobilization and participation; (ii) Planning, research and evaluation; (iii) improved pedagogy; (iv) School/village-based programme; (v) institution building and building capacity; (vi) Integrated education for the disabled; (vii) Innovations; and (viii) Monitoring and supervision.

All these interventions, directly or indirectly, are correlated with effective primary schooling which has to be understood in terms of the extent to which children learn what they are supposed to be taught in the school, Thus, student learning out comes constitute the primary measure for determining the quality of primary education.

All these interventions were supposed to influence the quality of schooling to varying extent. The DPEP inputs, based on needs and requirements of the specific social and developmental contexts, influence three major sets of correlates of learner performance *viz.* :

(i) Family characteristics;

(ii) School characteristics; and

(iii) individual characteristics.

With all these interventions put in place, it is expected that primary schools of DPEP districts would be tuned into better performing schools. As per the provisions of the DPEP Guidelines, it is obligatory that the effectiveness of DPEP interventions is to be assessed after a period of three years of their implementation.

Orissa joined DPEP in the second phase in 1996 with Bolangir, Dhenkanal, Gajapati, Kalahandi and Raygada districts coming under coverage. Three more districts namely, Bargarh, Keonjhar and Sambalpur came under the DPEP umbrella in 1997. DPEP in these eight districts are being funded by the world Bank. The programme has been upscaled to eight more districts: Koraput, Malkangiri, Nawarangpur, Boudh, Kandhamal, Maurbhanj, Nuapada and Sonepur with DFID support. Six more districts are in the pipeline. Thus 22 out of 30 districts are under the DPEP movement. The following are the major interventions mounted in the districts:

(i) Massive awareness generation programmes. Latent variant being the 'NINAD' launched during 2000-2001;

(ii) Preparation of districts plans based on micro-planning and consultative processes with genuine participation of all stakeholders;

(iii) Capacity building of teachers in new pedagogy-activity based, child centered, participatory, gender sensitive classroom processes;

(iv) Empowering VECs, MATs, PTAs and other such grassrouts level structures for effective participation in school management;

(v) Building for the buildingless schools, construction of additional classrooms, cluster Resources centre, Block Resources centres, toilets for boys and girls, provision for drinking water, undertaking major and minor repairs to school buildings;

(vi) Creating provision of schooling for school-less eligible habitations, alternative schooling centres for hard to reach groups of children; (vii) Creation of State Resource Groups (SRGs), District Resource groups (DRGs), and Block Resource Groups (BRGs), and building their capacity through training and exposure visits to other states and innovative projects;

(viii)

Improving school situation with the help of Rs. 2000.00 P.a 'school improvement Grants' and 'Teacher Grant' of Rs. 500/- per teacher per annum for developing teaching aids;

(ix) Specific interventions for girls and women, tribals and children with specific needs;

(x) ECCE as a major ready-to-school programme;

(xi) Strengthening the material and human Resources base of DIETs for training, monitoring and supervision and research with a long term prospective for sustainability of reform and renewal initiatives;

(xii) Improving learner performance through a multitudes of interventions such as improved school infrastructure, new pedagogy, better teacher performance, gender sensitive process and practices better curricula and text books etc.;

(xiii) Multi-pronged supervision to ensure those schools function efficiently and effectively.

All these intervention and initiatives were directed, in short, towards reforming and renewing the primary education system in five first phase DPEP districts.

Two major studies that have been planned to be taken up in DPEP context are: (i) Baseline Assessment study (BAS); and (ii) Mid-term Assessment survey (MAS).

As stated earlier, DPEP interventions and strategies planned for implementation during the project period are based on, among others, findings of research studies. Of these studies the BAS was singularly devoted to assessing students' achievement in two major subjects, namely language and mathematics. This study was intended to establish benchmark in respect of infrastructural facilities, students' characteristics, teachers and teaching-learning processes, and more particularly, learner achievement. This study also provides a basis for comparison between the established benchmark in the initial year of the project implementation and the situation that obtains at the end of the third year due primarily to the research-based interventions in DPEP districts. In short, BAS serves two important objectives: first, it establishes the existing levels in respect of a few critical indicators of school quality; and second, it provides a basis for comparison and indicates the improvements that have taken place over the measured baseline levels during a period of three years.

The BAS was conducted in five initial DPEP districts of Orissa, namely, Bolangir, Dhenkanal, Gajapati, Kalahandi and Rayagada in 1996. The findings of the BAS were used to identify the area of specific interventions to realise the goals of DPEP.

As per the stipulation of the World Bank Report (1994), the assessment studies are to be carried out during the third and sixth year of the project. The mid-term Assessment Survey (MAS) serves as a mid-way check point to examine if the planned intervention strategies are moving in the right direction yielding positive results. Precisely, MAS intends to :

(i) Assess the quantum of wide-ranging activities being carried out in different operational areas,

(ii) Identify areas which require additional or different inputs,

(iii) Apotlight pockets, hitherto, unknown and unexplored which require special treatment, and

(iv) Assist in applying mid-course corrective measures.

The DPEP has been proposed as an integrated approach to co-ordinate, consolidate and accelerate the quantitative as well as qualitative aspects. Quality of education stems from the quality of achievement of the learners who constitute the focal point in any learning system. The major components of quality of education could mainly be clustered under three groups of correlates, namely, (i) the level of material and human inputs or the characteristics of factors that go into the education process, (ii) the process itself *i.e.,* actions involved in school functioning, and (iii) the out come of the process *i.e.,* learner achievement in terms of their performance capabilities. The nature and extent of interaction between the first two *i.e.,* the inputs and process influence the third, namely, learner achievement (Govinda and Varghese, 1992). The quality of a school or an educational system should, in real sense, be judged in terms of learner achievement, namely, how much and how well the students have acquired the intended curriculum inputs (Dave, 1991). With this framework of the concept of quality of education, it would be worth examining the quality of primary schools in Orissa in its pursuit of UEE.

The DPEP, Orissa focuses on improving the access, and participation of 6-11 age group children so that all such children, irrespective of their place of origin or the socio-economic background, are able to complete quality primary education within stipulated period. To what extent these objectives have been realised? Which type of districts gained more as compared to other districts? What is the relative gain among the learners across their sex, caste and location in these districts? Study of this kind is quite essential in the context of Universalisation of Primary Education.

STATEMENT OF THE PROBLEM

The phenomena like under achievement, access, equity, dropout, stagnation have been causing a serious concern to educationists, and educational planner for several decades as it leads to affect the rate of literacy of the country as well as the state. It is considered as a block in the way of UEE. This necessitates serious probe into the causes that underlie and factors that lead to affect the achievement, quality, access and equity at primary level. So that means could be devised to handle with this serious problem.

Three are so many questions coming to the mind as regards the level of primary education in Orissa.

Are the special measures taken by Government yield a positive result?

- Has the achievement of the children of project districts (districts in which the scheme of Government is being implemented) been improved?
- Do the programmes have any positive impact on the achievement of primary school children?
- Is it possible to develop the rate of literacy among girls and other minorities sections through the help of the special programme like DPEP?
- Is it possible to remove the disparities in the achievement at primary stage by enrolled children?

The answers of these questions are planned to be derived empirically with the help of the present study.

OBJECTIVES OF THE STUDY

The following objectives were set forth for the investigation:

1. To find out if there were any impact of DPEP, Orissa on the access of the primary school children of five DPEP districts, namely, Bolangir, Gajapati, Kalahandi, Dhenkanal and Raygada taking the Base line survey and data as parameters.
2. To find out if there were any impact of DPEP, Orissa on the retention of the primary school children of five DPEP districts, namely, Bolangir, Gajapati, Kalahandi, Dhenkanal and Raygada taking the Base line survey and data as parameters.

3. To assess the achievement of learners at the primary level of education in language and mathematics of those five DPEP districts as stated above on the BAS tests.
4. To study the differences among the learners of primary schools of those five DPEP districts (*i.e.,* Bolangir, Gajapati, Kalahandi, Dhenkanal and Raygada) due to gender, location and caste variations on the BAS tests.
5. To assess the performance of learners' achievement on the MAS in language and mathematics at the end of class 1 and at the end of penultimate class of primary schooling of those five DPEP districts.
6. To compare the achievement differences in regard to gender and social groups on MAS tests of those five DPEP districts.
7. To compare the average performance of learners' achievement on the BAS tests administered during the initial survey in 1996 with that of learners' performance on the same tests re-administered during MAS in 1999 of those five DPEP districts.
8. To compare the performance of learners' achievement on the newly generated competency - based achievement tests in language (*i.e.,* Oriya), mathematics and environmental studies at the end of class III and class V in the four DPEP districts (*i.e.,* Bolangir, Gajapati, Kalahandi and Dhenkanal) and three Non-DPEP districts (*i.e.,* Ganjam, Puri, and Balasore) of Orissa.

HYPOTHESES OF THE STUDY

Keeping in view the above objectives, the following hypotheses were formulated and tested under present study:

1. There is a positive impact of the District Primary Education programme, Orissa on the access of the primary school children of five DPEP districts, namely, Bolangir, Gajapati, Kalahandi, Dhenkanal and Raygada.
2. There is a positive impact of the District Primary Education Programme, Orissa on the retention of the

primary school children of five DPEP districts, namely, Bolangir, Gajapati, Kalahandi, Dhenkanal and Raygada.

3. There will be significant difference in the mean scores of achievement in Oriya language on the BAS test between: (i) boys and girls; (ii) rural and urban students; and (iii) SC/ST and Non-SC/ST students of those five DPEP districts of Orissa.
4.. There will be significant difference in the mean scores of achievement in numeracy on the BAS test between: (i) Boys and girls; (ii) rural and urban students; and (iii) SC/ST and Non-SC/ST students of those five DPEP districts of Orissa.
5. There will be significant difference in die mean scores of achievement in Oriya language on the MAS test between: (i) boys and girls; (ii) urban and rural students; and (iii) SC/ST and Non-SC/ST students of those five DPEP districts of Orissa.
6. There will be significant difference in the mean scores of achievement in mathematics on the MAS test between: (i) boys and girls; (ii) rural and urban students; and (iii) SC/ST and Non-SC/ST students of those five DPEP districts of Orissa.
7. There will be significant difference in the mean scores of achievement in Oriya language on the BAS test and MAS test between boys and girls of class I and IV of those five DPEP districts of Orissa.
8. There will be significant difference in the mean scores of achievement in mathematics on the BAS test and MAS test between boys and girls of class I and IV of those five DPEP districts of Orissa.
9. There will be significant difference in the mean scores of achievement in class III children of DPEP and Non-DPEP districts on the newly generated competency-based test in : (i) Oriya language, (ii) mathematics, and (iii) EVS.
10. There will be significant difference in the mean scores of achievement in class V children of DPEP and

Non-DPEP districts on the newly generated competency-based test in :

(i) Oriya language,

(ii) Mathematics, and

(iii) EVS.

OPERATIONAL DEFINITIONS OF THE KEY TERMS USED

The key terms which have been used in the study are operationally defined here:

(i) District Primary Education Programme (DPEP)

The District Primary Education Programme (DPEP) is an effort to decentralize educational planning at the district level suiting the educational needs and demands of the particular district, with a view to achieving universal primary education, not only in terms of number and coverage, but also in terms of retention and attainment of the desired levels of learning by the children. It intends to renew and reform the existing primary education system in its quantitative and qualitative dimensions: access and enrolment, retention and quality and relevance. With DPEP interventions and inputs put in place, it is expected that the existing state of primary education, from both supply and demand perspective, in DPEP districts would substantially improve as envisaged in the DPEP guidelines (GOI; 1995). Three major planks on which DPEP rests are: first, community empowerment; second, improved classroom processes that are interactive, participatory, gender sensitive and child-friendly; and Third, transformed and effective primary schools with substantially higher levels of learner achievement. Here DPEP would mean the District Primary Education Programme in Orissa. DPEP was launched in the state with five districts, namely, Bolangir, Dhenkanal, Gajapati, Kalahandi and Rayagada coming into its fold in the year 1996. Subsequently, the programme was upscaled to another three districts: Baragarh, Keonjhar and Sambalpur in 1997. The programme is being upscaled to eight more districts: Koraput,

Malkangiri, Nawarngpur, Boudh, Kandhamal, Maurbhang, Nuapada and Sonepur with DFID support.

(ii) Access

Provision of schooling facilities within easy walking distance of all children is a pre-requisite for achieving universal access. Provision of access is an important aspect of universalisation of elementary Education (UEE). Expansion of primary education includes growth in the number of primary schools, increased school places to accommodate more and more school-age children, rise in the number of educationally and professionally qualified teachers, preferably women teachers and SC/ST teachers.

Hence, the term 'access' has been entertained here in terms of the expansion of primary education as stated above.

(iii) Retention

The main focus of planning for the development of primary education is concerned with enrolment, retention, and completion. Retention and completion are more important than enrolment. Efficiency of the system of primary education depends upon the completion of primary education of the children. Retention and Completion depend on the effectiveness of the system of school. Enrolment in the absence of survival figures, does not indicate the internal efficiency of the primary education system. Therefore, retention and completion rates are more revealing of the school effectiveness. Retention of children enrolled is function of demand for and supply of primary education. Here retention would tend to mean the survival figures of school-going children enrolled in the system of primary education.

(iv) Achievement

Achievement refers to the performance of a student in the school subjects. It tends to mean knowledge attained or skills developed in the school subjects usually designated by test scores or by marks assigned by teachers or both. According to Wiley and Andrew (1955) one of the main purposes of measuring the achievement of pupils is to ascertain the degree to which the educational objectives of the school are being realized. The results of the measurement of achievement, taken at intervals over a period of years, provide a continuous means of evaluation the students growth and help to determine the effectiveness of the curriculum in meeting the individual needs.

In the present study, achievement is operationally defined as the percentage of marks obtained by the learners in language (*i.e.,* Oriya) and mathematics for base line Assessment study (BAS) and mid-term Assessment survey (MAS). However, in case of the comparison of the DPEP and non-DPEP districts, achievement refers to the percentage of marks obtained by the learners of class III and V in three areas of learning, namely, language (*i.e.,* Oriya), mathematics and environmental science on the competency-based achievement tests prepared by the investigator.

(v) Primary Grade

The primary schooling encompasses the lower primary school (*i.e.,* from classes I-V) and the upper primary school (*i.e.,* from classes VI-VIII). However, the present investigator has restricted his study to classes I to V of the existing structural pattern of primary schools.

(vi) Impact

The concept 'impact' corresponds to the influence of the district primary education programme (DPEP) on the cognitive behaviour of the learners. It is evident from the scholarly literature that the DPEP exerts significant amount of influence on the learners, attendance and achievement. Looking from the learners' point of view, it can lee said that students through their increased participation learn a great deal and achieve more due to DPEP interventions, and are influenced. 'Learning' and 'getting influenced' are two dimensions of behavioural change; and again the change is assumed to be positive or incremental in nature. Hence impact here connotes a state of change or gain in quantity and quality (*i.e.,* as reflected in access, retention and achievement of learners at primary stage).

DELIMITATIONS OF THE STUDY

The scope of the study has been limited to its area, method, sampling, tools and techniques of the study. The study has been delimited in the following ways.

1. The study is confined to three major variables. *i.e.,* access, retention and achievement.
2. The study has been conducted in four DPEP districts like Bolangir, Kalahandi, Gajapati and Dhenkanal and three Non-DPEP districts like Ganjam, Balasore and Puri districts of Orissa.
3. The study has been conducted on 1000 DPEP students and 500 Non-DPEP students.
4. Achievement of students on two subjects like mathematics and language (*i.e.,* Oriya) has been taken into consideration while comparing the BAS and MAS. On the other hand achievement of students in three subjects like mathematics, language (*i.e.,* Oriya) and EVS has been considered while comparing the DPEP and Non-DPEP districts.
5. A competency-based test in mathematics and language (*i.e.,* oriya) and EVS carrying 25 marks each were prepared.
6. The sample for the Non-DPEP districts was drawn from Ganjam, Balasore and Puri districts of Orissa only.
7. A descriptive research method (survey method) has been used in the present study.
8. Statistical techniques like t-test and percentage were employed to analyse the data.

3

REVIEW OF RELATED LITERATURE

The review of the research literature pertaining to the problem of study becomes essential for the researcher in order to have a complete and thorough information of the work done in his country and abroad. The area of District Primary Education Programme (DPEP) is relatively a new field of study in the country.

In the present research the investigator has scanned most of the relevant and reported studies done in India and abroad in this field or related to the field. The present chapter provides a thumb nail account of such studies, their ambit and out comes. The available researches, which have direct or indirect bearing upon the project in hand; have been presented under two heads:

(a) Studies Conducted Abroad, and

(b) Studies Conducted in India.

STUDIES ABROAD

Achievement of students have always fascinated and attracted foreign researchers in the field of education and psychology. Some of the important studies are given below.

Prowden Report (1976) in the United Kingdom and Coleman *et al.,* (1977) in United States reported that neither school nor human and material resources makes a difference in learner's academic achievement. Factors that accounted for variations in test scores were family background characteristics. Socio-economic status, Parent's social class. Education and occupation.

Family environment and Locus of control. These factors were also found to be significantly correlated with academic achievement.

Schiefelvein and Simmons (1981) reported that availability of text-books, setting of homework and socio-economic status were related to higher student achievement.

The study by Heyneman and Loxley (1983) of science achievement at primary stage in 16 developing and 13 developed countries concluded "... Predominant influence on student learning is the quality of the schools and teachers to which the children are exposed".

Smith and Cheung (1986) conducted a study on the Philippines primary schools children and found out that the occupational and educational level of the parents had shaped the school attainment of their children.

Fuller (1987) while reviewing 50 studies identified length of the instructional programme, pupil feeding programmes. School library activity, years of teacher training, textbooks and instructional materials as effective parameters influencing school achievement.

Bósker and Scheerens (1989) conducted a study on between-school variation in achievement across countries. The study revealed that:

1. About 9 to 12 per cent of between-school variance for such studies.
2. The average for the group countries is 47 per cent at primary level.
3. There is greater heterogeneity in achievement between schools in developing countries than in developed countries.

Pollitt (1990) reported a significant relationship between protein-energy nutritional status and achievement test scores in china, India, Kenya, Nepal, Philippines and Thailand.

Cheng (1996) conducted a study on the effect of class room environment an students satisfaction and academic achievement and suggests that classroom climate and management style contribute differently towards different aspects of satisfaction or achievement.

Heyremanm and Sepulveda (1991) reported that availability of instructional material positively influences learned achievement the level of infrastructure seem to have a close correlation with learner achievement. Availability of text books and instructional materials has a consistently positive effect on learners achievement in developing countries.

Lockheed and Verspoor (1991) found that school-based interventions raise student achievement: The level of infrastructure seems to have close correlation with learner achievement as one moves from least facility schools.

Ross and Postlethwaite (1992) indicated the quality of education developed in a national study of primary schools in Zimbabwe. It provides a good version of a 'school effectiveness' approach.

The subject of the study includes school buildings, teachers and their living conditions, and school and classroom provisions. Schools were chosen with probability proportional to the size of the grade 6 enrolment, stratified by region, rural/urban and Government/Non- Government schools. About 20 pupils chosen at random from sixth grade at each of the 150 school selected.

The findings of the study include the differences in the inputs to the most effective and least effective schools were then studied as well as the correlation between inputs and achievement.

Serpell (1993) described that: (i) policy generally formulated has certain strategic advantages, but these are gained at a price which should not be regarded as inevitable, (ii) the criteria for monitoring and evaluation of a "schools" performance need to be expanded to include accountability to its local clientele, if the cycle of dis-empowerment of marginal communities is to be broken, (iii) what is required is a 'Learning process approach' which emphasizes the primacy of impact at the small-scale level.

The study of Cheng (1994) aims at investigation how classroom environment is related to students satisfaction and academic achievement in a sample of classroom in Hongkong primary schools.

The findings suggest that:

(i) satisfaction and academic achievement if students are strongly related to most of indication of classroom environment,

(ii) satisfaction and academic achievements have different sensitivity to different aspect of classroom environment,

(iii) to students satisfaction, social climate, class master's professional power (negatively) and position power (negatively).

The study of Dalin (1994) revealed that:

(i) success is much more widely determined that the relatively limited to students outcomes used as measure of school effectiveness in the quantitative tradition,

(ii) qualitative tradition is the importance given to the different prospectives on the change process from the different levels,

(iii) there seems to be a trade-off between the depth of information and the availability of reliable indicators in studies of school effectiveness and school improvement. Fuller and Clarke (1996) focussed on the culturally constructed meanings attached to instructional tools and pedagogy.

They argue convincingly for 'culturally situated model of school effectiveness' but talk at defining its new methodology.

The findings of the study were:

1. Under some conditions schools effects on achievement are greater than family background influences within impoverished setting.
2. School effects finding help to distinguish factors that are more consistently related to higher achievement.
3. Private schools do appear to out perform government schools in certain settings.

4. Instructional tool and even teaching practices are seen as cultureless, technical instruments for raising achievement.
5. Central policies hold a greater potential in touching the quality of instruction and the achievement of students.
6. There exists a significant effect of trained teacher and availability of text books on the school effectiveness.

Heneveld (1994) reported that: ranking of schools as a means of monitoring a national quality of education based on the presence of conducive conditions is entirely different from ranking effective schools based on the relationship of such conditions to pupils outcomes.

The Namibian National Learner Baseline Assessment (Namibian Ministry of Education and Culture, Florida State University, and Harvard University, 1994) produced new information on schools that could enable them to compared with others on the basis of English and Mathematics proficiencies.

The sample of the study include 137 primary schools from which all students in one randomly chosen Grade IV class and one randomly chosen Grade VII class were given criterion-referenced English and Mathematics tests developed to serve as BAS instruments.

The study was intended:

1. To construct school-level intake adjusted measures from the data set in the hopes of "disentangling the influence of (i) family and community factors, verses (ii) various school characteristics on learner achievement.
2. To link learner achievement data with information on local communities.
3. About two-third of the variation can be attributed to between school differences.
4. About 34 per cent of the variation in English achievements is due to child's background, refers to the proportion of total variation in achievement. And not the between school variation.

5. The use of positive outlying schools holds particular promise to understand the relative role of school, and family/community.
6. The study focussed primarily on the distribution of physical inputs to different schools and ultimately the relationship of such input to students reading achievement.

The major findings reported by Alexander (1995) in his study were:

1. A combination of quantitative and qualitative research in to classroom action yields considerably more than either qualitative or quantitative research on its own.
2. Teacher is to apply a similar mix analysis to their own planning and action.
3. Written work marked after the lesson provides at best incomplete evidence about pupils thinking process.
4. Interaction with the child while they are on task enable the teacher to enter and engage directly with those processes.
5. Accurate diagnosis of learning needs and accurate assessment of learning outcomes, free from preconceptions, is every child's right.
6. There is the need for much keen or commitment to time management within the classroom.
7. Teacher's scarce resources of attention and time can be used as efficiency and economically as possible.
8. Teacher's achieve a high ratio of work to routine/ disciplinary interactions and their pupil attain a high ratio of work to awaiting attention/distracted.
9. The test text carries its own 'motivational power' is grounded in careful research into children's thinking and learning process : Bert (1996) concluded that; (i) there will be in-and outside interventions and these interventions within the school and within classrooms disturb firm statement about stability; (ii) the size of the

school effect are uncertain; (iii) systematic differences in attainment between schools for different pupil groups is related to the problem in the measurement of the effects themselves and to the factors that can induce differential affects; (iv) these are almost no differential effects for schools with respect to socioeconomic and ethnic background in primary education; (v) in case of differential effect exist, they are related to intelligence or prior attainment; (vi) the differential effects could not be explained by school and classroom characteristics, but are partly explained by the method for language and mathematics used in the school; (vii) there are small differences in the slopes between schools with respect to prior attainment; (viii) these is little evidence that differential effects exist, *i.e.,* specific schools and classroom are not better for different group students.

Bert *et al.,* (1996) conducted a study entitled "Development in Educational Effectiveness theory and Research in the Netherlands". In this study, the development of a comprehensive model of educational effectiveness is described. The key factors of quality, time and opportunity are elaborated at all educational levels (student's, classroom, school and educational context).

The study deals with the following questions:

(1) What are the effects of configurations of school level and classroom level characteristics of students achievement?

(2) Are there any differential effects of school and classroom level characteristics on student achievement in schools with different types of student populations?

(3) What are the effect of school level and classroom level of characteristics on metacognitive skills of students?

(4) How stable are the effects of schools?

The main conclusions of the study are the following :

(1) Some of the characteristics at the classroom and the school levels in the Creemers model show the positive effects on achievement. Sometimes negative effects are found.

(2) There is instability of effects of characteristics across different dependent variables and across school subjects.

(3) There is some empirical support for the consistency principle at the classroom level and at the school level.

(4) More consistency does not lead automatically to higher effectiveness in terms of students achievement,

(5) Opportunity to learn and time for learning are the core variables of the model.

(6) Differential effects do occur in different categories of schools, dependent on the composition of student population in terms of socio-economic background and ethnicity.

(7) Time for learning is especially important in schools with disadvantaged student population.

(8) The 'tradition' effectiveness characteristics are important for the development of metacognitive skills.

(9) The effectiveness of school is not very stable across grades and schools years. Teacher effects are more substantial than school effects, although teachers are not necessarily effective for all subjects.

Creemers and Vandder (1997) reported that : (i) the amount of voluntary work conducted by parents had a positive effect on student achievement; (ii) from community participation negative effects are also apparent, like parents involvement in educational measures and signing home work by parents; (iii) community participation is an important concept to take into account the theoretical models of educational effectiveness in developing country; (iv) the-effect of the teacher professional development component, is the strongest; (v) variables at classroom level are not only relevant in western countries but also in development countries; (vi) community participation is cost effective, though its effect is very small; (vii) community participation is important when education become more decentralised and the community is held more responsible for the quality of the school careers of children. Strong parental involvement does not automatically lead to positive efforts on student achievement and sometimes when is a feature of poor-performing schools.

Mphuthi and Adeola (1998) drew the following conclusions from their study on "Learning organisation and the effectiveness of primary education in Lesotho" :

(1) It is important to take account of differences in students intake when studying the effectiveness in schools.

(2) Even when differences in intake have been taken in to account some schools arc more likely than other to lead to good outcomes.

(3) Some schools are better able to foster progress than are others. In some cases, the pupil intake to the less effective schools appears more promising.

(4) Some schools are more effective in fostering progress in some aspects of learning. Other may be more effective in others.

(5) Having a head-teacher who is purposeful but neither too authoritarian nor too democratic and who is able to share ownership of the school with colleagues is important.

(6) Pupils are involved and can be reworded on their efforts is important.

(7) Controlling behaviour with methods that are neither too weak not too harsh is likely to be most effective.

(8) Treating pupils with dignity and encouraging them to participate in the organisation of school gives a positive signal that they are valued.

(9) Keeping systematic records of pupils progress is crucially important if the curriculum is to have coherence for individual.

(10) Endeavouring to achieve a consensus on the values shared by the school as a whole needs to be a fundamental aim.

(11) Shortage of qualified teaching staff.

(12) High teacher-pupils ratio resulting in overcrowded classrooms.

(13) Inadequate or lack of school building facilities culminating in poor teaching and poor result which showed a decline in the rate of progress of pupils when compared to ten years back.

(14) Truancy, irregular attendance of pupils and lack of cooperation and understanding of parents in this regard hampered the school management and also contributed to the poor performance of such pupils.

(15) Irregular inspection of schools by the Ministry of Education inspectors which has led to the significant reduction in standard.

(16) Poor performance in English language, which is the medium of communication from standard IV in all subject except Sesotho (National Language).

The study of Tiguryera (1999) revealed that: improvement in school effectiveness was operationalized through workshops, on the job training, lesson observation, post observation, conference, demonstration lessons, collaborative planning, material production and use. School effectiveness is increased by promotion of active teaching and learning, creation of conducive learning environment, production of low cost material, introduction of collaborative group work, formulation mission statements, introduction of libraries, continuous assessment and establishment of school-based staff development, culture and teacher's resource centre etc. Sustainability of improved effectiveness could be achieved by empowerment of teachers and by collaborative effects.

Glewwe *et al.,* (1999) conducted a study on the "determinants of achievement in Jamaican Primary Education".

The findings of the study indicates that :

(i) All three components of physical and pedagogical inputs, pedagogical practices, and school organisation and climate influence student achievement;

(ii) There are much differences within each type of schools;

(iii) The difference in performance of students in an average all-age school compared with that for a student in an average primary schools is about one and half grade-levels.

The results of the study of Kularatna (1999) indicated that:

(1) There is a positive effect on knowledge, status of health, nutrition in children, improvement in knowledge and skills related to agriculture.

(2) The approaches adopted in the project greatly improved the standard of education in small, deprived primary schools.

STUDIES IN INDIA

A number of efforts have been made, in the past, by the Indian scholars to study the achievement of children at primary stage. The first major study on achievement in mathematics by Kulkarni (1970), revealed: boys achieved higher than girls; socio-economic conditions of the parents positively related with pupils achievement; privately managed schools provided better teaching-learning situations; and no relation was found between achievement and teacher qualifications. Dave *et al.,* (1988) in their study conducted in 22 states/UTs also observed larger differences in mathematics and language achievement of primary school children studying in class I to IV between states.

Nagaraju, (1992) conducted a study on intervention for MLL attainment in multi-grade contexts. The sample of the study included 184 rural schools of Karnataka state. A battery of achievement test was conducted in Kanada, mathematics and EVS., to at least three randomly selected students from each school.

The conclusions of the study were:

(1) There is a significant shift in the pattern of achievement in the case of change in performance of the children in their second year in both mathematics and language.

(2) In mathematics, the performance of children of first year showed a distributional change. But the gain was not statistically significant. About 10 per cent of the schools have other reference books and 80 per cent of the schools have charts, maps, globes, and other teaching aids.

(3) Every class has its own blackboard, chalk, duster and room duster.

(4) About 70 per cent of the schools are situated next to U.P. schools and hence share the facilities of common playground.

(5) About 50 per cent of L.P. and U.P schools are constructed in a school complex.

(6) Children do not dropout of L.P schools despite their participation in domestic and agricultural workforce.

Asthana (1993) reported the following results:

(1) With regard to sociological correlates, adjustment with examination and curriculum was found to be a significant correlate of dropouts of all groups.

(2) The dropout students felt more problems including adjustment, homework, timetable, in attending school and were less satisfied with classroom teaching as compared to non-dropout counterparts.

(3) There exists a significant relationship between socio-economic factors of the family and dropouts.

(4) Parental encouragement and atmosphere of the family were found to be significantly correlated to dropout phenomena.

(5) Non availability of adequate library, reading room, non-receipt of scholarship, unacceptable school tradition, prejudices and taboos were also correlated significantly to dropout.

(6) For parents the main reasons of dropout include proverty, sex-biasness of the society and difficult course content.

(7) For teachers dropout was due to property, low educational status and low awareness of parents, sex discrimination and difficult subjects.

Jangira, (1994) synthesized the results of BAS of seven DPEP states. The major findings of the study were:

(1) Students performance was low in reading as well as in mathematics.

(2) There existed a significant difference in achievement across the schools as well as across the states.

(3) The individual level predictors for language achievement were educational and occupational aspiration, watching T.V. receiving dictation and feed back on tests, opportunity to read.

(4) For prediction of mathematics achievement, the individual level variables were fathers occupation, fathers education, reading other materials, correlating home-task regularly and educational and occupational aspirations, etc.

Jangira, (1994) reported that the individual level predictors for language achievement were educational and occupations aspiration, teacher coming to class regularly, T.V. watching, receiving dictation and feed back on tests, opportunity to read materials other than test books, language and availability of text books.

For prediction of mathematics achievement, the individual level variables were fathers education, reading other material, correcting homework regularly, educational and occupational aspiration and understanding teachers language.

For mathematics achievement, class size and teachers expectations were found to be significant predictors.

The study of Shukla (1994) revealed that over the states, the difference between the mean achievement of boys and girls did not have the same direction. In some states boys did better than girls whereas in some other states girls did better than boys. In all the states the SC/ST pupils performed lower than the non-SC/ST ones. Further, the pupil's achievement was found to be positively related with father's education, facility for learning and educational environment at home. The variables related to schools and teachers indicated somewhat weak relationship with achievement.

Agarwal and Harding (1995) found that: (i) there is no functioning community based school management body such as parent-teacher association; (ii) although enrolment may be high, attendance is low, and the time children spend on the responsibilities given to them after interferes with time that is supposed to be spent in school; (iii) communication are poor, and the system of supervision is not functioning in an effective or supportive manner, (iv) teacher need further support in the development and use of activity based teaching methods, (v) many students attending schools are in poor heath, and are not well-fed. Limiting their potential to participate fully in the classroom; (vi) however gender gap is not statistically significant; (vii) girls perform better in government schools than in private schools in language; (viii) performance of girls in Government schools is as good as or marginally better than boys; (ix) socio-economic background of students exerts a positive influence on learners achievement. The effect size is large and statistically significant; (x) organization of teaching-learning activity is seems to be a significant variable both in terms of effect size and statistical significance.

Ambasht and Rath (1995) studied the effect of household, community and school factors on the enrolment, retention and achievement of ST children at primary level and reported that: (i) there is significant effect of the occupation of parents with that of the enrolment; (ii) no preschool facility is available; (iii) tribal dialect as medium of instruction is not used in schools except very few cases; (iv) qualification of teacher is largely higher secondary and above, most of the teachers are trained; (v) low income group has less participation of children in school; (vi) tribal language is not reported to be the medium of instruction and therefore, this perhaps could be one of the causes for non-attendance; (vi) training is in pedagogy and no training in tribal life or tribal culture is provided; (vii) community participation is lacking perhaps because of Village Education Committee does not exist; (viii) very few parents participate in school functions; (ix) reasons for dropping out are predominantly illness which throws light on the state of affairs in health programmes; (x) mean score of incentives due not establish that incentives are casual factors for high retention; (xi) timely availability of the facilities is responsible for high retention; (xii) household factors like parents education, fathers occupation, mothers occupation, help received from family, availability of enough, food etc. effect the achievement of students; (xiii) no factor showed any significant relationship with mathematics or language achievement except reading newspaper on language achievement; (xiv) academic help from the family was found to be significant in the achievement of mathematics and language; (xv) homework has significant effect on achievement of mathematics.

Jain and Arora (1995) conducted a study on 'effect of school level variables on achievement gap between boys and girls' and found that:

(1) There is achievement gap between boys and girls.

(2) The achievement gap increases in both language and mathematics after controlling the pupil level variable in most of the states and it has negatively associated with the achievement.

(3) The achievement gap in mathematics is larger than language.

(4) Students perform better in the expended primary schools than the primary schools.

(5) Presence of more than 50 per cent female teachers in a school is likely to improve the performance of girls.

(6) The frequent assignment of mathematics problems is negatively associated with the achievement gap between boys and girls.

(7) Teachers commitment and leadership of headmaster has made a positive impact on the learning achievement of children.

Nayar (1995) conducted a study on gender issues in primary education. The major findings were:

(1) The problem of access obtains in small sized village and scattered habitations. Availability of education and other development infrastructure of health, ICDS, water, electricity, roads, women's development groups/ programmes is almost nil in villages with population less than 100 and increases with population size of the villages. Villages with 1000 or more population are better endowed and have higher levels of literacy and schooling facilities at least up to middle and even high school level;

(2) Very large villages have a problem when even two primary schools do not suffice and some valuable sections are left out.

(3) Urban slums are worst off and rarely have a school if it comprises recent migrant from villages.

(4) There is evidence of a growing demand for girls education.

(5) Girls are not sent outside the villages. Primary Education would become a dead end for girls unless commensurate facilities are created at the middle level. Middle schools were located at 3 to 8 km. Distance from smaller villages.

(6) Enrolment ratio for girls at the primary level very from 80 per cent to 116 per cent.

(7) Drop-out rates for girls are very high and invariably higher than those for boys, exception Kerala.

(8) Phenomenon of non-enrolment of elementary age groups is very high in Madhya Pradesh but is considerable elsewhere except in Kerala.

(9) Drop-out takes place largely after a girl is about 10+ or after primary for lack of middle school.

(10) Majority of households were poor/low income households in Madhya Pradesh. There were a very small proport on who had annual income above Rs. 12,000/-.

The study of Rath and Saxena (1995) revealed that : (i) SC/ ST students scored lower than non-SC/ST students in both the subjects; (ii) fathers education contributes for better achievement of SC/ST students; (iii) in mathematics, the achievement gap does not vary significantly across the schools where as in languages it vary significantly in Karnataka and Kerela; (iv) tests and feedback provided by teacher tends to reduce the gap between SC/ST and non-SC/ST Students in language.

Reddy (1995) reported that : (i) the physical and cultural environment of home and neighbourhood of children, particularly of the non-enrolled an dropout children who belong to the disadvantaged groups are not conductive for promoting the required entry behaviour of children to survive in school; (ii) social and cultural reforms and interventions are the prerequisite for educational development of the disadvantaged children; (iii) parents are rarely contacted by the teachers to motivate and persuade them to sent heir children to school; (iv) there is readiness on the part of the community to respond and support the educational programme but not able to realise their aspirations; (v) both parents and children have negative image of the teachers and they also developed negative image of the school; (vi) there seem to be no body to help the boys and girls to send them to school; (vii) poor achievement levels of children seems to be an important reason for losing faith and interest in schools; (viii) because of pressure of work at home the children are irregular to school and poor in studies, so the parents would like to withdraw them from school; (ix) the chance of boys and girls sustaining themselves in schools beyond the age of 8 years is difficult as it is at this age they become potential full time workers, where the economic conditions of the families help to reinforce this potential; (x) parents who feel that primary education (class I-V) is not functional for them as it can not give them extra employment opportunities; (xi) children are not able to sustain themselves in schools because of dull and drab learning transaction. They find it difficult to sit through the whole day in the school. There is hardly any enjoyable activity besides the poor environmental condition of the school; (xii) teacher do not care to pay any attention to the school. They keep away the children at a distance. Teacher do not do anything to improve the cleanness and habits of children. The cultural gap is not bridged.

Roy *et al.*, (1995) found that:

(1) The mean scores for language, mathematics and EVS were much below the minimum expected scores (MES).

(2) The students of government schools from socio economically privileged section of society scored higher in all the three subject, than the other group.

(3) For urban and rural students and for boys and girls, there was hardly any difference in achievement.

(4) Impact of mother's education on learner's achievement appeared to be greater than father's education.

(5) Students from small families also-performed better than moderate or large size families.

The study of Senapathy (1995) indicated that; there were significant differences in the cognitive development levels and mastery of concepts in environmental studies across urban and rural samples. The rural and slum children were not very different. Universalisation of elementary education would not be complete with greater allocation of money and building funds. What's required is the reorientation of the content and process to suit the local diversities.

Shukla (1995) undertook a study to find out the effectiveness of various interventions for improving tribal education. The findings of the study were; (i) the DPEP states have planned various interventions for education of tribal children which can be classified under following categories.

(1) Academic and education facilities.

(2) Stipends/Attendance scholarships.

(3) Welfare interventions.

(4) Interventions/Incentives for teachers.

(5) Ashram schools.

(6) Miscellaneous including tribal hostels. Boarding grant, subsidised hostels etc.

Singh and Saxena (1995) conducted a study on the effect of school policies and practices on students achievement.

The study revealed that: (i) the association of teacher qualifications with school mean achievement is not consistent across states. It is positive in two of the states (Assam and Tamilnadu) and negative in other two states (Kerala and Madhya Pradesh); (ii) the teaching experience is negatively associated with mathematics and language achievement; (iii) the in service teacher training is also negatively associated with achievement for mathematics (in Karnataka) and language (in Kerala); (iv) the factors of educational and physical facilities in schools have positive association with school mean achievement in mathematics. These associations are mostly consistent across states; (v) the number of teacher and pupil teacher ratio have negative association with achievement; (vi) teacher qualification is negatively associated with gender achievement gap in mathematics, where is it is positively associated with language achievement gap; (vii) period of stay has provide, negative association in mathematics for Madhya Pradesh. But positively associated in Karnataka, and negative in Orissa for language achievement gap; (viii) in service training has" .indicated positive association with language achievement gap; (ix) access to teaching material for mathematics in Assam and percentage of female teachers for language in Madhya Pradesh, Orissa and Tamilnadu tend to reduce the gender achievement gap; (x) SC/ST students score lower than non SC/ST students, because of their personal background; (xi) teaching experience tends to widen the gap where as parents involvement, test and feed back tend to reduce the gap; (xii) the OB scheme has shown a positive and statistical significant impact on achievement in mathematics and language; (xiii) in Karnataka free text books has indicated negative association with language achievement; (xiv) Assam has indicated positive impact of attendance scholarship in language where as Kerala has impact of the scheme for both subjects.

Singh and Saxena (1995) conducted a study on achievement difference and school effects.

The study attempts : (i) to study the effects of school related variables on pupil's achievement using the data of baseline assessment studies conducted in eight states of India; (ii) to study teacher's quality, school resources and school academic climate are studied after adjusting pupil's background and school context variables.

The finding of the study were:

(1) The achievement in mathematics varies substantially, within schools from the highest 80 per cent in Kerala to the lowest 39.4 per cent for Karnataka. In language the corresponding position is 86.3 per cent for Kerala and 54.8 per cent for Karnataka.

(2) Mostly the within schools variances are uniformly lower in mathematics than the language.

(3) Variation in achievement between schools for mathematics and language for each state are statistically significant.

(4) There are large and statistically significant differences between boys and girls within schools in their achievement in mathematics. These differences are also found statistically significant in language achievement for most of the states.

(5) There are large and statistically significant gap in mathematics achievement of SC/ST and non-SC/ST students except Haryana, Orissa and Tamilnadu. In language achievement the gap was statistically significant in Haryana, Kerala and Madhya Pradesh.

(6) Father's education within the schools has shown a positive and highly significant association with pupil's achievement in mathematics and languages in all the states except Karnataka, Maharashtra and Tamilnadu for mathematics and Haryana for language. Similarly, mother's education has displaced highly significant association with achievement except Tamilnadu for mathematics, and Karnataka and Tamilnadu for language.

(7) The differences between pupils who have related one or more grades, and those who have not, are large and statistically significant.

(8) At the school level the mean SES is positively associated with the achievement in mathematics and language after adjusting for pupil's background.

(9) The association of teacher qualification with the school mean achievement is statistically significant in Assam and Kerala (mathematics and language), in Maharashtra (mathematics), in Madhya Pradesh (language), and in Tamilnadu (language). It is positive only in Assam and Tamilnadu.

(10) The in service teacher's training is negatively associated with achievements for mathematics (in Karnataka) and language (in Kerala).

(11) Duration of stay of teacher in the present schools tends to be positively associated for mathematics in the state of Madhya Pradesh and for language in Tamilnadu.

(12) Tacher giving arithmetic problems to solve in the classroom regularly, contribute significantly at 1 per cent level to the mathematics school mean achievement.

(13) Teacher commitment is positively associated for mathematics in Maharashtra and for Language in Haryana, Madhya Pradesh and Maharashtra.

(14) There is large differences between boys and girls in their achievement and these differences very across the schools. The variation in these differences is uniformly lower in language, than that of mathematics.

(15) There are large differences between SC/ST and non-SC/ST students in their achievement.

(16) Teaching experience is negatively associated with mathematics and language achievement.

Varghese (1995) found that: (i) about 86 per cent of the total variance is accounted by within schools factors and remaining 14 per cent is accounted by between school factors; (ii) about 80 per cent of the variance in mathematics achievement score is accounted by within school factors; (iii) an analysis of achievement difference between government and private school shows that between school variance is less in Government sector than in private sector in both language and mathematics achievement; (iv) Government schools are more similar among themselves than the private schools; (v) there is scope for improving school effectiveness if actions are taken at the school level; (vi) girls have a marginal achievement disadvantage in language.

Gupta and Gupta (1995) studied the effect of state interventions on pupils achievement and found that; (i) the O.B. scheme had shown a positive and significant impact on mathematics and language achievement in the state of Assam, Kerala, and Madhya Pradesh after controlling for the effects pupils background variable; (ii) the effect size of the OB scheme on mathematics and language achievement was found to be positive but not significant in the state of Karnataka, Orissa and Tamilnadu; (iii) in Haryana and Maharashtra the mean performance was relatively low in OB schools as compared to non OB schools; (iv) the effect size of the OB scheme become significant after controlling the effect of contextual variable, in Assam on mathematics, achievement, in Kerala on Language achievement and on mathematics and language achievement in Maharashtra; (v) the items supplied on OB scheme had contributed significantly towards improving pupils achievement in the state Haryana, Karnataka and Madhya Pradesh; (vi) supply of free text books had positive and significant impact on both mathematics and language achievement in Madhya Pradesh where as provision of mid-day programme in school had significant effect on language achievement only. Scholarship for regular attendance had a positive and significant impact on language achievement in Kerala.

Chakarabarti and Sharmistha (1996) made an attempt to find out the impact of non-detention policy on dropout rates and achievement level of children and its relevance to the effective implementation of DPEP. The sample of the study were 1608 students enrolled to class I during the academic sessions 1974 to 1988. The subjects were selected from four schools belonging to Magrahat one Block of south 24 Parganas (district).

The findings of the study were:

(1) Dropout rate at class III was higher as compared to class I and II.

(2) Dropout rate was lower in second phase (1984-88) as compared to first phase (1974).

(3) Percentage of girl's dropouts were higher as compared to boys.

(4) Mere declaration of non-detention policy was not enough to reduce stagnation and drop-out rate.

Goel (1996) reported that the performance of students at representational level was better than their performance at abstract-level. Students performed better at concrete level than representation and abstract levels. The learning problems as related to arithmetic difficulties as identified included memory problems, reading problems, language problems, cordinality problems, symbol confusion, lack of the concept of place values, inability to subtract and lack of mastery on computational skills.

Gupta *et al.,* (1996) concluded that: The school profile presented a sad tale as regards the effects of shikshak samakhya, availability and filling up of vacant post of teachers. Most of the teachers teaching in multigrade setting did not have any pre-service training. The teachers felt the need for psychological continuity in class distribution. Teachers were not accustomed to use the blackboard. Teachers were not concerned about curriculum organization strategies and timetable strategy for enhancing students participation. Only 20 per cent students in grades I and II and 33 per cent in grade III, IV and V were found regular. Improvement of students attainment was observed during the experiment across all setting and grades.

Kapoor and Upadhy (1996) conducted a study on Numeracy and reading readiness level of entrants to class I.

The study identifies: (a) reading readiness and numeracy readiness level of entrants to class I, (b) components of readiness which need strengthening, (c) relationship between readiness levels of entrants to class I and teachers rating on child's social maturity, (d) relationship between environmental factor and readiness level and (e) to provide feed back to curriculum planners and text book writers.

The result revealed that: (1) Vast majority of children lack adequate level of readiness for reading and number work at the time of entry to school. (2) Poor performance was shown with regard to sequential thinking, serration, space concepts and pre-number concepts. (3) Children with preschool experience had better readiness level. (4) Academic readiness was also found to be highly related to physical, psychomotor and socio-emotional state of development of children. (5) Enhancing school readiness of children, pre-school programme for all children, and preparing text books to help children acquires specific skills for improving reading and numeracy readiness levels would help in improving the learning achievement of children at the primary stage.

Khader (1996) conducted a study on empowering primary teachers for effective classroom transactions in DPEP school.

It was concluded that: (i) classroom transaction dominated by direct presentation and teacher talk, and the use of child centered activity based approach was found to be considerably less; (ii) at the teachers training level, conventional approach assumed centered stage of the transaction mode marginalising activity based interactive mode of transactions; (iii) multigrade school groups were well differentiated by three factors Classroom Management, Planning instructional activities. Instruction for learner involvement; (iv) from strategic planning perspective, multigrade and non-multigrade schools needed training inputs to improve classroom management, planning instructional activities and instruction for learner involvement with foci on activity based hands-on experiences and practical skills; (v) there existed dependency syndrome among teachers in the sense that they lacked perception of their professional rules in finding solution to the academic problems they confronted and sought prescriptive solution from trainers or authorities.

Lakasmi (1996) conducted a study on impact of school readiness programme on primary school children and concluded that:

(1) Children who took part in activity-based learning showed significant difference in skills related to language, number and cognitive areas.

(2) The attendance of children in experimental schools improved considerably.

(3) Experimental schools with ECE background scored well both in Mid- term and final evaluation.

(4) Rate of decline in dropout rate was significantly lower in experimental schools as compared to controlled schools.

Prakash and Panda (1996) found that :

(i) there was a large variation in the mean performance of students across the DPEP states, although in over all, language performance was better than mathematics; (ii) area and gender did not influence the mean performance of students in both mathematics and language;

(iii) the overall situation across and within states at the lower primary stage appears to be very alarming;

(iv) level of performance of students of Assam, Orissa and Haryana was relatively higher than the students of Tamilnadu, Maharashtra and Madhya Pradesh;

(v) the performance of the students in the test of language, was almost identical in respect of state of Orssa, Assam, Haryana, Maharashtra and Madhya Pradesh;

(vi) performance of students in Tamilnadu has been significantly much lower than the performance of students from other states;

(vii) average performance of class II students in language has been found to be relatively better than the average in mathematics;

(viii) average performance of the students of Tamilnadu was not only lowest in mathematics and language but also far below than the average performance of the students from the rest of the DPEP states;

(ix) average performance of the boys was a little higher than that of girls across all the DPEP states, but these difference were not statistically significant both in mathematics and language.

Rath (1996) conducted a study on the effect of schooling process on learning outcome. The findings of the study were:

(1) There were 29 per cent and 20 per cent variance across the school of mathematics and language, respectively where as for self-esteem and attribution process, it was 10 and 12 respectively.

(2) Within the school, girls performance in mathematics and language was not different from boys. However, it was not consistent across the school in mathematics.

(3) Students of backward category were performing lower in mathematics and language than general category within the school but varied significantly across the school in mathematics only.

(4) SC students performance was less than general students in mathematics within the school they had lower self-esteem than general students within the school but not consistent across the schools.

(5) Meta cognitive awareness of the students appeared as a significant determinant of mathematics and language achievement and their self-esteem with the school.

(6) Family environment of students was found to have substantial effect on mathematics and language achievement at school level as a contextual variable.

(7) On average, school with better mathematics achievement also had better language achievement.

(8) At the school level, attribution process was strongly related to mathematics achievement where is self-esteem was with language achievement.

(9) Pupils perception about their teachers, head teacher's co-operation to teacher in the management of academic matter, pupils inclination towards trenchers had discernible effect on mathematics achievement of

students, where as mathematics qualification of teachers had negative impact on the same outcome.

(10) Percentage of female teachers, pupils inclination towards teacher, instructional approach in classroom, head teachers concern for students significantly influenced the language achievement.

(11) Class size, students- performance to work in groups, sequential presentation of lesson with comprehensible language and instructional approach in classroom improved the self-esteem of student's substantially, where as closeness among teachers negatively influenced the self-esteem.

(12) Head teacher's cooperation to teachers in the management of academic matter and group feeling among students, attributed positively towards the attribution process of students.

Senapathy (1996) reported that: (i) there was no equity in the performance of urban, rural and slum children on both piagetian tasks and competency-based tests; (ii) urban children were in a more advantageous position as compared to their rural and slum counterparts; (iii) performance in all the groups was much below the desired level.

The study of Singh and Saxena revealed that:

(1) There were large difference between-boys and girls in their achievement. These differences varied across schools. The variation was uniformly lower in language than that of mathematics.

(2) There were large differences between SC/ST and non-SC/ST students in their achievement.

(3) Parents education and fathers occupation had a positive association with pupils achievement and were mostly consistent across the states.

(4) Teaching experience was negatively associated with mathematics and language achievement.

(5) During of teacher's stay in the school tended to be positively associated with pupils achievement.

Reddy (1995) studied the status of primary education in the web of proverty culture particularly in the context of the non-enrolled and dropout children. The study attempted to probe into and assess the exiting physical, social and cultural environment of the home, neighbourhood and communities particularly of non-enrolled children and dropouts.

The major findings of the study were:

(1) The physical and cultural environment of home and neighbourhood of non-enrolled children belonging to the disadvantaged group were not conductive for education.

(2) Parents were neither approached nor motivated and nor persuaded by teachers to send their children to school.

(3) Low achievement level of children was major reason for losing faith and interest in school.

(4) Children were unable to attend the school as both the parents had been working and these children were required to attend to the domestic chores and look after siblings.

A study entitled "Determination of learner's achievement at primary stage" by Singh (1996) attempts to study the determinants of learner achievement at primary stage using data of Karnataka state base line assessment survey covering 177 schools, 442 teachers and 2568 pupils.

The objective of the study was to determine the learners achievement at primary stage by re-analyzing the Base line Achievement Study (BAS) data of one state, namely, Karnataka.

A multistage stratified random sampling procedure was followed in the selection of sample. The sample comprised of 30 students of class IV, 5 teachers from each of 30-35 primary school from each of 4 districts of *i.e.,* Belgaum, Kolar, Mandya and Raichor (with female literacy rate below 39 per cent as per 1991 census).

The major findings of the study were: (i) there were large and significant differences between schools in their mean performance; (ii) government schools performed lower than the privately managed schools; (iii) on average girls were performing lower than the boys but in some schools girls were performing better; (iv) the SC/ST students were performing lower than the non-SC/ST students and these difference did not very across schools; (v) there was a positive association between mean-SES (in take composition) and school mean performance.

Singh and Bala (1996) made an attempt to study the role perception of VEC members of DPEP districts in Haryana and the findings were:

(1) There was significant difference between proposed and actual number of VEC members.

(2) Significant difference was found in expected and perceived role of VEC members.

(3) The perception regarding the 13 enlisted roles of VEC with regard to 50 per cent and above to be performed by Grampanchyat than VEC.

(4) Incase of 14 enlisted roles of VEC in mobilizing community participation for UPE it was found 50 per cent and above in case of only three roles, *i.e.*, (i) motivate villagers to sent all the children of 6-11 years age group to school; (ii) to keep continues contact with community for achieving the target of UPE and (iii) contact the parents of dropouts to regularize them.

(5) Item-wise analysis revealed that in general all the nine expected role under the dimension of school function of VEC towards villagers in general were perceived as a role of VEC than other agencies by the member belonging to all categories.

Srivastave (1996) conducted a study parents and teachers perceptions of gender related-issues for improving access, enrolment, retention and achievement of girls at primary stage.

The objectives of the study were: (i) to understand the view points of parents and teachers on gender and gender related issues; (ii) to find out how both parents and teachers together can play a crucial role in encouraging girls education.

The findings of the study were:

(1) Women teachers of both the school belonged to Hindu religion.

(2) About 90 per cent of women teachers were married.

(3) About 25 per cent of the women teachers were between 35-40 years of age group.

(4) About 45 per cent of the women teachers had an annual income of more than one lakh rupees, this depicts that the economic standard was fairly good.

(5) About 35 per cent of women teachers had a teaching experience of ten to twelve years followed by 30 per cent had experience five to ten years. Women teachers came from fairly good socio-economic and educational backgrounds.

(6) All the parents agreed that parent teacher meeting can help in increasing parents involvement in school activities.

(7) Parents felt that parent teacher meeting can help in achieving the goal of UPE (Universalisation of primary Education).

Also the results of the study indicated that access, enrolment and retention of girls in primary schools can be improved significantly if: (i) parents and teachers have a positive attitude towards gender and gender related issues; (ii) non-discriminations is followed between boys and girls in teaching-learning process, extra curricular activities sitting arrangements appointment of monitors etc.; (iii) parents treat both sons and daughter equally and (iv) simultaneously socio economic and educational background of parents are improved through social and economic interventions.

Srivastave (1996) conducted a study on DPEP teachers training programme (Madhya Pradesh and Maharashtra). It was found that:

(1) The SCERT training programme emphasized child centered and learning centered teaching.

(2) Story telling, poetry, songs, plays, group games, toy making, creative activities, body control exercise, manipulation of objects and pictures were used for teaching in lower classes.

(3) Dakshasikshan package stressed on MLL competencies and their evaluation.

(4) Maharashtra had a 3-tier training system. Viz: SCERT-SRG and DRG-BRG—teachers and head masters.

(5) Training programme in Maharashtra concentrated on: (i) competency backed teaching; (ii) joyful learning; (iii) material development; (iv) planning; (v) girls education; (vi) puppetry; (vii) action research.

(6) Training in Madhya Pradesh includes; (i) competency based teaching; (ii) school readiness programmes; (iii) personality development through individual and group activities.

The study of Barapanda (1997) revealed the following findings:

(1) The rate of enrolment increased from 36 per cent in 1991 to 100 per cent in 1996.

(2) The rate of retention scaled up from 14 per cent in 1991 to 93 per cent in 1996.

(3) The 7 per cent dropout was due to of migration of parents.

(4) Among girls, 97 per cent had been able to avail the opportunity to study primary stage.

The study of Duhan and Punia (1997) revealed that: (i) children had their language performance below average; (ii) the environment provided at school or home was not conducive for language development; (iii) performance on comprehension and expressive aspects was very poor; (iv) it was found that children were not exposed to variety of activity or materials which could help them in their development, even activities like story telling or poem recitation were not regularly performed which help in expressive aspects of language; (v) teaching aids were not prepared and used by any teacher; (vi) none of the teachers was self motivated but worked under compulsion and did not take initiative in the performance of activities; (vi) none of the teacher narrated stories but a majority recited poems/ rhymes frequently; (vii) no one encourage individual child to narrate events and other activities for language development.

Lakshmi (1997) reported that:

(1) Children who took part in activity-based learning in experiment schools showed significant difference in skills related to language number and cognitive areas.

(2) The attendance of children in experimental schools had improved. The activity oriented joyful learning motivated the children to attend the school regularly.

(3) The difference between control and experimental school continued up to the final examination even if experimental-based learning technique had not strictly been continued in all schools.

(4) As for as cognitive/number skills are concern 't' ratio is not significant, at the stage of final evaluation.

(5) Two experimental schools with ECE background scored well both in mid-term and final evaluation. They were continuously exposed to activity oriented approach.

(6) Rate of decline in drop-out may be less in the case of experimental schools, yet it is significant in terms of the trend, as we notice an increasing trend of drop-out rate in the control schools.

Padhi *et al.*, (1997) reported that parents education and fathers occupation were positively associated with pupils achievement.

Rath and Kumar (1997) suggested that: (i) all outcome measures varied substantially across the school; (ii) metacognitive awareness of students, family environment and ability of students influence significantly for achievement in mathematics and language; (iii) ability of student was found significant in addition to metacognitive awareness and family environment; (iv) language achievement was significant influenced by pupils inclination towards teacher, academic activity in classroom, and head teacher's concern for student matter; (v) students performance to work in group and sequential presentation of lesson with understandable language significantly influenced the self-esteem of students.

Sahoo (1998) reported the positive influence of social factors on the achievement of students in mathematics and language.

Sharma *et al.*, (1998) conducted a study on the functioning of alternative schools in DPEP districts of Madhya Pradesh. The study was conducted with the following objectives:

(1) To identify the strength and weakness of alternative schools.

(2) To assess the enrolment and dropout status in alternative schools.

(3) To collect the opinion of teachers, supervisors, parents and community members about the functioning of alternative schools.

The study was confined to the six districts of Madhya Pradesh. About 120 alternative schools in the form of 12 projects were to be opened in the year 1995-96, but 112 alternative schools were actually started. The data for the study were collected from 37 alternative schools randomly selected from 12 Blocks, two /three were selected from each Block. It includes six districts.

Major findings of the study were:

(1) Out of 37 alternative schools under study, about 19 alternative schools (51.35%) are within the range of 10-20 km. from Block H.Q. About 5 alternative school (13.31%) are at a distance of 20-30 km. Whereas 13 (13.31%) are situated at a distance of more than 30km. from Block H.Q.

(2) The alternative schools were held either at a teachers residence, a community members residence or other places like temporary shed or under a tree etc.

(3) One of the reason for dropout was found to be improper and disputed venue of the alternative school.

(4) The timning of holding the schools were left at the discretion of the concerned clientele. Majority of the schools were held from 11. a.m. to 3 p.m. morning and evening were kept free for children to look after their domestic work.

(5) Out of the total student enrolled 17.3 per cent were S.C, 34.5 per cent S.T. and 39 per cent OBC and only 9.2 per cent belonged to the general category. About 42.8 per cent of total strength was found to be girls.

(6) Although, Teaching Learning Material (TLM) was supplied in 80 per cent of the schools studied, but it was not sufficient. TLM was not supplied in time inspite of repeated request.

(7) As many as 52.7 per cent of the parents are illiterate and only 7.3 per cent have studied up to Sr. Secondary. About 69 per cent are engaged in agriculture and 21 per cent belong to Labour class.

(8) About 31 per cent parents expressed non-suitability of the venue of alternative schools, 16.4 per cent exprėssed co-education as the main reason for not sending their children to alternative schools, 36.6 per cent parents says they need help in supplementing the family income, 34.5 per cent of parents have said education is not related to their needs. Some of the parents (10.9 per cent) indicated that their children are afraid of the teachers.

(9) Inspite of various reasons given for not sending their children to school, majority of them (71 per cent) indicated their willingness to send their children to school while 19 per cent of the parents were not at all willing to send their wards to school.

Vasishtha and Madan (1998) conducted a study on the achievement in science and mathematics as a function of learning organization of competencies in mathematics at primary stage.

The study revealed that: (i) fifty primary stage MLLs competencies were identified as critical hard spots of learning primary grade students; (ii) standard IV of MLLs at primary stage was found to be the most difficult for students; (iii) the areas of mathematical learning, in order of decreasing difficulty were IV, III, II, V and I; (iv) highly significant positive relationship were found to exist between mastery/non-mastery on selected primary-stage MLL competencies in mathematics mastery of MLLs seems to lead to high achievement in mathematics in subsequent years and non-mastery acts as a deterrent; (v) highly significant positive relationships were found to exist between mastery/non-mastery on primary-stage mathematics competencies and achievement in science; (vi) sex difference were found to be non-existent so far as highly significant positive relationship between mastery of MLL competencies and achievement in mathematics and science were concerned.

Aggarwal (1999) conducted a study entitled, "A comparative analysis of Access and Retention in DPEP and non DPEP districts". The objective of the study was to develop profiles of DPEP districts in terms of; (i) growth of enrolment; (ii) repetition rate for each class and (iii) gender and caste based differential in enrolment.

The subject of the study includes 42 districts of seven DPEP states and were treated to specially designed computer software.

The findings of the study were:

(1) Increase in enrolment was calculated in 1996-97 over the base years 1993-94.

(2) Index of gender equity and index of social equity used in the study reflected only on the level of inequalities and not on access or retention.

(3) A consistency pattern in enrolment and retention of children including girls, SC and ST children.

(4) Positive gains in enrolment were shown by alternative school (AS) and Education Guarantee Scheme (EGS) in Madhya Pradesh.

(5) The efforts made to improve in DPEP districts have been successful.

Behera and Das (1999) conducted a study on "Effect of learning corner activities on learner's achievement".

The aims of the study were: (i) to conduct learning corner activities by teachers with various classroom strategies like pair work, group work, paper tutoring etc.; (ii) to installed a resource room containing locally available competency-based teaching-learning material, to be effectively used by the teachers for conducting learning corner activities.

The conclusion of the study was that there is a significant gains in all the four curricular areas like mathematics, language, EVS-I and EVS-II.

Gupta *et al.,* (1999) conducted a study on learning achievement of children studying in alternative schools of DPEP districts of Madhya Pradesh.

The study examined the learning achievement of children in language and mathematics in 30 alternative schools in six districts of Madhya Pradesh.

The results of the study were:

(1) The low mean scores of children in simple statement-type items in mathematics were strong indicators that there was very little emphasis on understanding the concepts.

(2) Children were found committing mistakes of 'matras' and other grammatical mistakes.

(3) Though teaching-learning material was available in all the schools, but it was not in an adequate quantity.

(4) Children fared well in the one on writing numbers in increasing order than in the one on writing numbers in decreasing order.

(5) Problems of understanding the local dialects by the investigator, long distances of alternative schools from the Block and the district H.Q. resulting in poor monitoring, may be some of the reasons for the poor performance.

(6) There was no significant difference in the learning achievement of girls and boys, but on the whole there

was a significant difference and still it was in favour of the girls.

(7) In the achievement of Hindi language, girls were found better placed than the boys on the whole.

(8) The performance of children in mathematics was found to be better than in Hindi language in all the districts.

The study of Khatua *et al.*, (1999) revealed that: (i) mastery learning strategy was more effective compared with the teacher-centered approach in enabling learners to attend mastery of competencies in mathematics; (ii) children with rural background were found better than urban ones in attaining mastery in a few competencies; (iii) background class children were superior than general caste learners in the use of calendar and understanding the concept of divisions; (iv) learners belonging to small size classes performed better than their counterparts in large size classes in at least five competencies; (v) learners in small-size classes were superior to those from multigrade classes in some competencies; (vi) the attainment of mastery in five competencies was found better in multigrade context than in large-size classes.

Lakshminarayana *et al.*, (1999) conducted a study on motivation and classroom practices as indicators of school effectiveness. The study was designed to find out the relationship between primary teacher's motivation and their classroom practices. It also examined the influence of certain demographic factors like gender, educational qualifications, teaching experience, type of school and location of school on teacher's motivation and classroom practices.

The study was conducted on a sample of 224 teachers drawn from 68 primary schools in one DPEP and one non-DPEP district of Andhra Pradesh.

The findings of the study were:

(1) There is a positive relationship between teacher motivation and classroom practice.

(2) The non-DPEP district teachers were found to be more motivated than DPEP district teachers.

(3) Gender influenced the classroom practices, while education qualification of teachers influenced both the motivation and classroom practice.

(4) The study could not established any influence of teaching experience, and the type and location of schools on both motivation and classroom practices of primary school teachers.

The study of Nair (1999) attempted to compare the sub-dimensions of classroom climate and the total classroom climate of DPEP and non-DPEP primary schools of Kerala state. The classroom climate of 188 classrooms from DPEP district and 216 classrooms of non-DPEP districts was observed.

The findings revealed that the classroom climate in the DPEP classrooms was better than the non-DPEP classrooms in selected schools. The DPEP intervention strategies like regular in-service training, teacher-support material, regular monitoring and supervision etc. were also found helpful in minimizing certain classroom situations that deliberated achievements.

Pradhan (1999) undertook a study on the effect of home and school related factors on learning achievement in mathematics of class V children of primary grade.

The study revealed that home factors have positive effects on enhancing mathematics achievement.

The study of Prakash *et al.*, (1999) attempted to appraise student's achievement during Mid-term Assessment Survey under DPEP.

The main objectives of the study were:

(1) To measure the students average achievement in language and mathematics at the end of class-I and at the end of penultimate class of primary schooling.

(2) To camper achievement on the BAS tests of 1994 and 1997.

(3) To camper achievement differences with regard to gender and social groups.

(4) To examine the relationship of home, school and teacher variables on students achievement.

The study revealed that: (i) all the districts of Assam, Haryana, Karnataka, and Kerala and 9 districts of the remaining states need crossed 60 per cent level of achievement in language and mathematics in class-I; (ii) students performance in mathematics compared with language in class-I showed significant improvement in BAS tests, however, in class-III BAS tests showed decline in mathematics compared with language; (iii) The DPEP goal of reducing gender inequalities in achievement in class I was accomplished in a majority of districts, where as the urban-rural and SC/ST differences in achievement were, realised in about 50 per cent of the districts; (iv) in service programmes in all districts of Kerala, Assam and a few in Madhya Pradesh have shown incremental influence on teaching of mathematics and language.

Srivastava (1999) conducted a study on the internal efficiency of primary education in phase-I DPEP districts.

The objectives of the study were:

(1) To find out the extend of wastage in primary education.

(2) To study the effect of dropout rate and repetition rate on internal efficiency.

The study revealed that: (i) in 18 districts internal efficiency was good, as expenditure was not more than 25 per cent, implying no wastage of resources; (ii) in 13 districts where internal efficiency was satisfactory, expenditure was between 25 per cent and 43 per cent; (iii) in the remaining 9 districts internal efficiency was poor, since the expenditure incurred was over 43 per cent; (iv) the dropout rate was lowest in Kerala *i.e.,* below 2 per cent and was as high as 50 per cent in few districts of Assam and Madhya Pradesh; (v) majority of states, *i.e.,* 19 out of 23 districts, have shown improvement in the retaining rates except Madhya Pradesh; (vi) DPEP districts have achieved a perceptible success in enhancing access, enrolment, retention and reduced inequalities, specially among girls, SC and ST children; (vii) DPEP districts have also witnessed a reduction in the wastage.

Das (2000) found that primary school children had severe learning difficulties in the area of number and the four fundamental operations.

Panda (2001) Conducted a study on the indicators of quality learning achievement of primary school children in Orissa.

The major objectives of the study were:

(1) To find out the present achievement level of rural primary schools students in different school subjects in the state of Orissa.

(2) To find out the present academic performance of urban primary school students in different school subjects in the state Orissa.

(3) To find out the present academic achievement status of tribal Primary school students in different school subjects in Orissa.

(4) To camper the academic performance of rural, urban and tribal primary school student in Orissa.

(5) To find out the influence of home factors on academic achievement of rural, urban and tribal primary schools student in Orissa.

(6) To find out how school-related and teacher characteristics effect academic achievement among rural, urban and tribal primary school students in Orissa.

(7) To examine the influence of student's characteristics on academic achievement among rural, urban and tribal primary school students on Orissa.

(8) To camper the academic performance of rural, urban and tribal primary school students who have continuously. Completed studies from class-I to IV and are continuing class-V in different school subjects like mathematics, science, language and social studies in Orissa.

In the present study disproportionate stratified sampling design was used to collect the relevant data. Six districts, seven blocks, 64 schools, 245 teachers and 882 students out of which

478 boys and 404 were girls constitution the sample of the study.

The Major findings of the study were: (i) there is no significant effect of gender on learning achievement in relation to rural, urban and tribal students; (ii) caste base significant effect on achievement of mathematics in rural areas and all other areas and subjects are significant; (iii) it was noticed that non SC/ST Learners performed better in mathematics as compared to SC/ST learner; (iv) father education has shown significant effect on rural, urban and tribal areas. However, children of college educated fathers have shown better performance in rural and urban areas; (v) mothers education has significant effect on mathematics achievement in rural areas and mathematics and language achievement in urban areas. Children of mothers educated up to Higher Secondary level performed better both in rural and when areas as compared to illiterate mothers; (vi) income has significant effect on mathematics and language achievement in rural areas and science in urban areas Children of higher income families performed better in mathematics and language achievement In rural areas. Whereas children of middle income families performed better in science achievement in urban areas. There is no effect of father's occupation on learning achievement in all the three areas; (vii) availability of food has significant effect on enhancing learning achievement in tribal areas; (viii) tution does not have any significant effect on enhancing learning achievement in rural, urban and tribal areas in all the school subjects; (ix) gender has significant effect on mathematics and science achievement in rural areas; (x) children have performed better in mathematics and science in rural areas where male teacher taught in the school rather than female teacher; (xi) teachers qualification has significant effect on mathematics and language achievement in urban and tribal area respectively; (xii) students have performed better in mathematics and language where higher qualified and CT trained teacher teach the subject; (xiii) infrastructural facility and learning achievement in all subject are significant in rural areas. Education facilities have significant effect on mathematics achievement in rural areas where as they are significant in all subject in urban and tribal areas; (xiv) home-work and correlation of the home-work have a significant effect on learning achievement in all subject in rural and rural and urban areas; (xv) preparation and utilization of teaching aids by the teacher has a significant effect on mathematics and science achievement in urban areas, and (xvi) incentive schemes have a significant effect on enhancing learning achievement in rural and tribal areas but not in urban areas.

THE PRESENT STUDY IN RELATION TO THE ABOVE LITERATURE

The review of the foregoing studies indicates that a number of researches have been conducted in the area of learners' achievement at primary stage. It is quite apparent from the findings of these studies that there is no consistency in the pattern of relationships between the achievements of pupils and other related variables. Achievements of students, particularly in Indian context, differ widely from school to school, and state to state. However, there is dearth of studies available which have direct bearing on the present investigation. It is therefore in fitness of things that the present study aims at filling a research gap by way of comparing the data on BAS and MAS (*i.e.*, in terms of access, retention and achievement); and DPEP and Non-DPEP districts.

4

DESIGN OF THE STUDY

"Scientific problem can be resolved only on the basis of the data and a major responsibility of scientist is to set up of a Research Design capable of providing a data necessary to the solution of his problem, while the unit of Research makes it impossible to say that one aspect is more crucial than another. The collection of data is of paramount importance in the conduct of research, since obviously, "no solution can be more adequate than the data on which it is based" (Mouly, 1964 p. 95).

The first and foremost requisite in any research is data without of which no study could be conducted. Hence, without data production research is not possible. For collection of data, the investigator has to set up the design, *i.e.*, to plan before hand, to explain the procedure used in the study, the investigator has to describe the technique used for collecting the data for his investigation. He has to describe the sampling method, the population, the sample, the tools used, the reliability and validity of tools used, the method adopted and the procedure employed in the tabulation and organisation of the data.

The previous chapter Review of Related Literature pertaining to the present investigation, precise formulation of the Research problem, relevant hypotheses, etc., have been discussed, keeping in view of the above fact the researcher felt it very essential to describe to the design of the study which includes a brief description of the followings:

1. Method of the study,
2. Population and sample,

3. Sources of collection of data,
4. Procedure for collection of data,
5. Data treatment.

METHOD OF STUDY

The present study has been planned and implemented under a Normative survey method. It aims at studying the impact of DPEP interventions on access, retention and achievement in primary grade. As such the ambit of the investigation was confined to a normative survey and analytical approach.

Hillway (1956) states that: "If the scholar can not clearly describe his method, the chances are that it is too vague and general to yield him satisfactory results." So, there is the need to describe the method used in research work, the decision about the methods depends upon the nature of the problems selected, the kind of data necessary and its objectives. Keeping in view of the above rationale the investigator has chosen the method for his study *i.e.,* so far as the research methodology is concerned, in the present study normative survey method has been used.

The term normative implies the determination of normal, or typical conditions or practices. The term normative survey, is generally used for the type of research that we intend to consider here—the research which purposes to ascertain what is normal or typical conditions or practices at the present time.

In the present study an attempt has been made to determine typical condition as regards the achievement in mathematics, Oriya language and EVS of project districts of Orissa.

POPULATION AND SAMPLE

A population generally refers to any collection of specified group of human beings or of non-human entities such as objects, educational institutions, time units, geographical areas or salaries etc. Measuring the entire population is impracticable though not entirely impossible. So one has to draw a sample from the population concerned.

Since the primary schools were the basic units of study, the universe consisted of blocks, schools and students of five DPEP districts namely, Bolangir, Dhenkanal, Gajapati, Kalahandi and Rayagada and three Non-DPEP districts namely, Balasore, Ganjam and Puri. In the present study sampled students of class III and class V were drawn from four projects districts namely, Bolangir, Dhenkanal, Gajapati and Kalahandi.

Multi-stage stratified random sampling technique was employed for selection of various subjects of the study namely. Blocks, Schools and Students.

At the first level, blocks were selected. It was decided to take at least one block from each district (both DPEP and non-DPEP). While selecting the blocks, die urban areas, if any, were excluded from the blocks. The list of blocks, arranged in alphabetical order, was prepared out of the total number of blocks in each district, one block was selected randomly.

At the second level, urban areas were selected, prior to selecting the urban areas, all the urban areas were arranged alphabetically. Only one urban area was randomly selected from among the listed urban areas.

At the third level, schools were selected from the sampled block and urban area using the table of random numbers from the list of schools. Only four schools (*i.e.,* two schools from a block and 2 schools from urban area) from each district (both DPEP and non-DPEP) were included in the sample (cf Appendix-I).

At the fourth level, the students of classes III and V were selected from the sampled schools. For class III, one section, if the school happened to have more than one section, was selected. If the number of students of the section was 20 or less, all the students were included in the sample. In case the number of students is more than 20, the names of boys and girls on roll were alternatively arranged and finally 20 students were selected using random start. On the other hand, for class V, a section was, if the school has more than one sections, selected. If the section has 30 or less than 30 students, all the students of the section were included in the sample. When the number of students was more than 30, the names of the boys and girls were alternatively arranged and then 30 students were finally selected using random start.

The distribution of sample students of class III and class V of DPEP and Non-DPEP districts on the basis of location, gender and caste has been given separately in Tables 4.1 and 4.2 respectively.

Table 4.1 : Distribution of Sample Students of Class III into Different Categories

DPEP Districts	Area	Boys		Girls	
		General	SC/ST	General	SC/ST
Dhenkanal	Rural	15	12	18	13
	Urban	21	9	24	11
Kalahandi	Rural	12	14	10	7
	Urban	16	8	19	6
Bolangir	Rural	10	9	8	11
	Urban	17	5	16	6
Gajapati	Rural	14	17	16	13
	Urban	18	10	18	8
NON-DPEP Districts					
Puri	Rural	23	12	17	9
	Urban	45	5	42	7
Balasore	Rural	21	8	15	5
	Urban	43	6	14	4
Ganjam	Rural	19	9	27	9
	Urban	13	11	48	9

A look at Tables 4.1 and 4.2 show that the number of districts (both DPEP and non-DPEP) blocks and schools selected and the number of students selected from each district in terms of gender, location and caste are broadly representative. Thus, in all there are 411 students from class III of DPEP districts (*i.e.*, rural General boys N = 51, rural SC/ST Boys N = 52, rural general Girls N = 52, rural SC/ST Girls N = 44, urban general Boys N = 72, urban SC/ST Boys N = 32, urban general Girls N = 77 and urban SC/ST Girls N = 31); 421 students of class III from Non-DPEP districts (*i.e.*, rural general Boys N = 63, rural SC/ST Boys N = 29, rural general Girls N = 59, rural SC/ST Girls N = 23, urban general Boys N = 101, Urban SC/ST Boys N = 22, urban general Girls N = 104 and urban SC/ST Girls N = 20); 426 students from class V of DPEP districts (*i.e.*, rural general Boys N = 30, rural SC/ST Boys N = 53, rural general Girls N = 104, rural SC/ST Girls N = 31, urban general Boys N = 58, Urban SC/ST Boys N = 28, Urban general Girls N = 89 and urban SC/ST Girls N = 33); and 438 students from class V of Non-DPEP districts (*i.e.*, rural general Boys N = 48,

Table 4.2 : Distribution of Sample Students of Class V into Different Categories

DPEP Districts	Area	Boys		Girls	
		General	SC/ST	General	SC/ST
Dhenkanal	Rural	9	13	29	8
	Urban	16	6	25	5
Kalahandi	Rural	7	11	25	6
	Urban	14	9	21	11
Bolangir	Rural	8	17	27	7
	Urban	15	3	16	4
Gajapati	Rural	6	12	23	10
	Urban	13	10	27	13
NON-DPEP Districts					
Puri	Rural	21	7	19	6
	Urban	57	9	32	6
Balasore	Rural	19	6	13	8
	Urban	54	7	28	81
Ganjam	Rural	8	5	24	9
	Urban	18	5	58	11

rural SC/ST Boys N = 18, rural general Girls N = 56, rural SC/ST Girls N = 23, urban general Boys N = 129, urban SC/ST Boys N = 21, urban general Girls N = 118 and urban SC/ST Girls N = 25) which may be considered adequate for determining the representativeness of sample of students of the study.

SOURCES OF COLLECTION OF DATA

To achieve the stated eight objectives (*i.e.,* 2.3.1 to 2.3.8) of the study, the data required were available from the sources mentioned here under.

Official Documents

Official documents like A Baseline Assessment study of primary schools in Orissa, 1996 and A Mid-Term Assessment survey in Orissa (Bolangir, Dhenkanal, Gajapati, Kalahandi, Rayagada), 1999 available in the office of the Directorate, T.E. and S.C.E.R.T., Orissa were collected school records (in case of DPEP districts) were examined in respect of students who had dropped out before the completion of the terminal stage of schooling.

Tools Used

For fulfilling die last objective (*i.e.,* 2.3.8) of the study, the following tools were employed for collection of data:

(i) Achievement tests in language, mathematics and EVS for class III.

(ii) Achievement tests in language, mathematics and EVS for class V.

(iii) Overview of the achievement tests for class III.

This is a comprehensive test which was developed to assess the learning achievement of class III children in different competencies of Mathematics, Language and EVS based on class III syllabus. It has three parts. The first part of the comprehensive achievement test was mathematics test. It consisted of 25 items of 25 marks. It covers the competencies like understanding of place value of 3 digit number, arrangement of 3 digit number in descending order, comparing 3 digit numbers using the sign, understanding of even and odd numbers, addition of two three-digit numbers, subtraction of three-digit numbers with borrowing, multiplication of two-digit numbers, division of three digit numbers, solving, simple money problems using division and multiplication of two digit numbers, understanding of relationship between meters and centimeters, understanding of relationship between standard units of measuring capacity (*i.e.,* liter and milliliter), calculation of surface area of rectangular regions using non-standard units, reading of clock by hour, interpretation of calendar, demonstration of understanding of the meaning of proper fractional numbers, as parts of regions with the numerator and denominator not exceeding 10, and conversion of fractions and mixed numbers to decimals and decimals to fractions and mixed numbers, with value up to two decimals places. All the items were presented in multiple-choice format. No time limit was kept for the test, but on an average, 30 minutes was taken to complete the mathematics test.

The second part of the comprehensive Achievement Test was Language Test. It consisted of 25 items of 25 marks. These items were divided into two sections. The first section, word meaning section, constituted of 10 items with equal number of antonyms and synonyms. The second section, intended to assess reading comprehension had 15 items presented in multiple-choice format to measure pupils' understanding of meaning of words and sentences and passages of factual details. The items were arranged in order of increasing difficulty. Correct response to each item was scored 1 mark. On an average the students took about 20 minutes to complete the language test.

The third part of the Comprehensive Achievement Test was Environmental Studies Test. Environmental Studies is one of the major subject areas at the primary stage. It aims at developing in the child an awareness and understanding of one's natural and social environment. This test contained 25 items in two sections. Items were presented in multiple choice format to measure pupils' awareness and understanding of natural and social environment, while constructing the test items, due consideration was given to different competencies, as suggested in M.I.L. for class III in EVS.

Overview of the Achievement Tests for Class V

This test was developed to assess the learning achievement of class V children in different competencies of Mathematics, Language and Environmental Studies.

The first part of the Comprehensive Test was Mathematics Test. This test was based on mathematics syllabus for class V consisting of 25 items presented in multiple-choice format. These items were intended to measure the pupils' understanding of four fundamental operations-decimal and fractional number, multiples, unitary method, measurement of time, weight and measures. Items, in this test, were also arranged in the ascending order of difficulty. Correct response to each item was awarded 1 mark. It took about 25 minutes to complete the mathematics test.

The second part of the comprehensive Test was Language Test which was based on class V syllabus on Oriya Language. The test contains 25 items which were divided into two sections. The first section, word meaning section, constituted of 10 items with equal number of antonyms and synonyms. The second section, intended to assess reading comprehension, had 15 items presented in multiple-choice format to measure pupils' understanding of measuring of words and sentences and passages of factual details, drawing inferences, and identifying central ideas. The items were arranged in order of increasing difficulty, correct response to each items was scored one mark. It took about 20 minutes to complete the language test.

The last part of the comprehensive Test was Environmental Studies Test. This test contained 25 items, which were divided into two sections. The first section, science, constituted of 12 items, while the second section, social studies, had 13 items presented in multiple choice format to measure pupils' understanding and awareness of natural and social environment. The test was based on class V syllabus on EVS. The items were prepared keeping in view the different relevant competencies suggested in M.I.L. for class V in EVS. The items were arranged in order of increasing difficulty. Correct response to each item was scored 1 mark. It took about 20 minutes to complete the EVS test.

Analysis of Items

The present study is intended to make a comparative analysis of achievement of classes III and V students of the sampled DPEP and Non-DPEP districts. The achievement tests on Mathematics, Language and EVS for classes III and V as discussed earlier were used for the purpose. It was considered necessary to make an analysis of the items contained therein in terms of the diagnostic value of the items.

For the above purpose, the Difficulty Index (DI) and Discriminative Power (DP) following the procedures as laid down in Gronlund and Linn (1985) have been determined. The Difficulty Index of test items is calculated by the formula R/T × 100. The Difficulty Indices of the times in competency-based tests are useful for use in the classroom.

It is obvious that the Difficulty Indices of the test items may vary from '100' to 'O' per cent. Usually, the DIS of 50% level on average are acceptable for achievement tests. The items having DIS within the range of 40% to 60% Difficulty Index values are considered to be of moderate difficulty (Gronlund and Linn, 1985) and are considered suitable for norm-referenced tests like the present ones.

The formula used for calculating the discriminative power more conveniently, runs as $R_U - R_L/½T$. The discriminative power may range from +1.0 to –1.0 indicating maximum positive discrimination and negative discrimination respectively. The discriminative power of an item is calculated on the basis of the difference between the proportions of learners in the upper and lower 25 per cents of the total group responding correctly to the item. This index is meant for differentiating between the high achievers and low achievers in the group. As such, the items, for the convenience of interpretation, have been classified under three broad categories such as good and very good, reasonably good, and marginal and poor having the DP values 0.30 and above, 0.20 to 0.29 and 0.19 and below respectively. Such DI and DP values for the items on Mathematics, Language and EVS tests for classes III and V have been presented in Tables 4.3,4.4 and 4.5 respectively.

The statistical values as given in Tables 4.3, 4.4 and 4.5 sufficiently provide us the evidence for the use of the tests.

Table 4.3 : Difficulty Index (DI) and Discriminative Power (DP) of the Items of Mathematics Test for Class III and V

Item No.	Class III		Class V	
	DI	DP	DI	DP
1.	86.82	0.45	92.14	0.52
2.	84.21	0.51	90.74	0.54
3.	80.44	0.48	69.13	0.86
4.	69.41	0.53	83.37	0.78
5.	62.33	0.43	64.84	0.82
6.	67.68	0.37	61.33	0.93
7.	69.24	0.61	59.75	0.71
8.	60.20	0.35	64.17	0.83
9.	80.11	0.78	68.31	0.79
10.	77.32	0.54	69.68	0.67
11.	84.05	0.33	74.17	0.78
12.	80.27	0.61	80.33	0.75
13.	68.63	0.39	82.56	0.82
14.	85.71	0.78	63.57	0.87
15.	74.37	0.73	87.52	0.68
16.	61.45	0.79	69.65	0.53
17.	76.13	0.65	65.24	0.44
18.	67.34	0.63	59.79	0.63
19.	74.37	0.81	68.25	0.71
20.	77.76	0.41	60.25	0.75
21.	73.75	0.47	61.29	0.84
22.	68.14	0.46	65.27	0.49
23.	84.09	0.37	73.84	0.53
24.	61.41	0.78	69.27	0.74
25.	62.35	0.49	63.84	0.82

Table 4.4 : Difficulty Index (DI) and Discriminative Power of the Items of Language Test for Class III and V

Item No.	Class III		Class V	
	DI	DP	DI	DP
1.	84.02	0.45	87.76	0.61
2.	83.19	0.54	85.33	0.68
3.	80.25	0.48	84.89	0.55
4.	73.17	0.51	72.36	0.81
5.	68.64	0.37	78.53	0.55
6.	90.21	0.59	87.61	0.44
7.	81.29	0.72	67.93	0.68
8.	60.54	0.74	83.54	0.56
9.	78.2	0.39	86.56	0.64
10.	67.59	0.54	71.60	0.82
11.	90.31	0.37	81.36	0.35
12.	91.02	0.48	81.05	0.33
13.	74.09	0.65	75.91	0.59
14.	61.45	0.76	84.59	0.56
15.	73.57	0.78	80.83	0.48
16.	80.15	0.77	72.96	0.36
17.	71.72	0.38	70.06	0.61
18.	84.35	0.72	74.84	0.58
19.	81.97	0.50	75.26	0.41
20.	76.88	0.89	69.44	0.72
21.	69.68	0.86	63.83	0.53
22.	67.29	0.77	69.81	0.41
23.	83.25	0.74	78.34	0.73
24.	84.89	0.88	68.14	0.54
25.	72.36	0.92	61.59	0.81

Table 4.5 : Difficulty Index (DI) and Discriminative Power (DP) of the Items of EVS Test for Class III and V

Item No.	Class III		Class V	
	DI	DP	DI	DP
1.	88.90	0.38	95.19	0.38
2.	80.56	0.49	90.01	0.44
3.	80.33	0.55	88.54	0.47
4.	84.39	0.39	83.17	0.42
5.	68.72	0.55	71.54	0.67
6.	69.67	0.78	78.37	0.41
7.	67.29	0.92	69.44	0.82
8.	77.48	0.88	80.41	0.54
9.	80.78	0.53	88.54	0.51'
10.	83.2	0.37	87.22	0.39
11.	87.59	0.54	90.15	0.61
12.	82.13	0.55	69.16	0.73
13.	69.68	0.74	80.78	0.44
14.	87.15	0.49	83.45	0.39
15.	73.68	0.38	64.24	0.53
16.	78.28	0.55	63.25	0.71
17.	84.26	0.41	83.10	0.43
18.	73.75	0.59	69.58	0.55
19.	76.29	0.38	72.05	0.58
20.	72.73	0.49	65.21	0.32
21.	80.50	0.44	68.99	0.77
22.	78.15	0.52	61.55	0.35
23.	70.97	0.39	71.57	0.58
24.	72,74	0.51	66.76	0.73
25.	80.19	0.62	69.53	0.48

PROCEDURE FOR COLLECTION OF DATA

As mentioned earlier, a set of newly generated competency-based achievement tests in Mathematics, Language and EVS for Classes III and V were employed for assessing students' performance. For the collection of data from the sample schools of DPEP and Non-DPEP districts, necessary permission of D.I. of schools was sought. The heads of the selected schools were contacted on the spot. The task of data collection was accomplished with the help of two field investigators who were given a short orientation as regards their activities and responsibilities during the time of data collection. The competency based achievement tests were administered to the sample students of classes III and V of the sample schools present on the day of data collection.

Necessary rapport was established through personal contacts. The purpose of the study was explained to them. Before administering the tests the general instructions with regard to responding the items were thoroughly explained. Each sample respondent was requested to respond all items of the tests sincerely. The respondent was assured that the responses would be kept strictly confidential. The students were asked to respond to each item of the tests and to proceed to the next item as soon as they completed one. The completed tests of each respondent was scored. Correct response to each item was scored 1 mark. After scoring the tests of sample students, the investigator organized the whole data, checked it to see the accuracy, utility and completeness. After editing, the data were classified and tabulated for the analysis according to the stated objectives (cf. Appendices IV)

DATA TREATMENT

The data were analysed with a view to assessing the current status of students' achievement on newly generated competency - based achievement tests in Mathematics, Oriya language and EVS for the classes III and V administered on the sample students of the sample DPEP and Non-DPEP districts of Orissa. For the above purpose, the statistical technique of 't' test was used.

5

ANALYSIS AND INTERPRETATION OF DATA

In the present chapter analysis, interpretation and presentation of results have been provided systematically. The focus of the study was to see the impact of DPEP, Orissa on the access, retention and achievement of learners in primary grade. The design and methodology employed for conducting the study have been discussed in the preceding chapter. In order to maintain the logical sequence and ease in presentation of results and formulation of findings, the whole analysis has been divided into six sections. The first section (A) deals with the study of the impact of DPEP, Orissa on the access of the primary school children belonging to the five DPEP districts as mentioned in the objective. The second section (B) is concerned with the study of the impact of DPEP, Orissa on the retention of the primary school children of the same DPEP districts. The Third section (C) brings fourth an assessment and comparison thereby of the achievement of learners at the primary level in language and mathematics of those five DPEP districts on the BAS tests. The fourth section (D) deals with assessment and comparison thereby of the achievement of learners at the primary level in language and mathematics of those five DPEP districts on the MAS tests. The fifth section (E) is concerned with comparison of the performance of learners' achievement on the BAS tests with that of MAS tests of those five DPEP districts. In the final section (F) an attempt has been made to study and compare the performance of learners' achievement on the newly generated competency-based achievement tests in Oriya language, mathematics and EVS at the end of class III and class V in the DPEP and Non-DPEP districts of Orissa.

SECTION A: STUDY OF THE IMPACT OF DPEP, ORISSA ON THE ACCESS

The first objective of the study was to find out if there were any impact of DPEP, Orissa on the access of the Primary School children of five DPEP districts, namely Bolangir, Gajapati, Kalahandi, Dhenkanal and Rayagada. In this connection, it was hypothesised that there would be positive impact of the DPEP, Orissa on the access of the primary school children of five DPEP districts as stated above. For the above purpose, the relevant BAS data have been taken as parameters. The term access has been operationally defined in Chapter II. In the present context, growth in the number of primary schools, increased school places and facilities to accommodate more and more school-age children and rise in the number of educationally and professionally qualified teachers, preferably women teachers and SC/ST teachers have been considered as the indicators of access. The relevant data pertaining to the access have been given in Table 5.1 through Table 5.4.

Table 5.1 : District-wise Distribution of Primary Schools

District	Number of Primary Schools		% of Increment
	1996	2001	
Bolangir	1702	1933	13.57
Dhenkanal	911	1115	22.39
Gajapati	803	937	16.69
Kalahandi	1450	1705	17.59
Rayagada	1372	1482	5.83

The entires made in Table 5.1 are very clear and self-explanatory. It can be observed that number of primary schools in the sample districts has increased (ranging from 5.83% to 22.39%) over the five years. The relatively faster increase in number of such schools is found in Dhenkanal district. Out of the five project districts, Rayagada has experienced the lower increase in the number of primary schools.

Table 5.2 : Distribution of the Percentage of Sample Schools having Essential Facilities

Facilities	Year	Bolangir	Dhenkanal	Gajapati	Kalahandi	Rayagada
Safe Drinking water	1996	17.78	20.00	31.43	14.29	43.24
	1999	42.00	54.00	52.00	32.00	44.00
Toilet	1996	20.00	20.80	8.57	4.78	43.24
	1999	20.00	38.00	8.00	16.00	38.00
Separate toilet for girls	1996	8.89	0.00	2.86	2.38	37.83
	1999	12.00	36.0	6.00	10.00	30.00
Electric current	1996	8.89	20.00	25.71	16.67	32.43
	1999	14.00	24.00	16.00	14.00	32.00
Chair for teachers	1996	3.17	22.34	26.05	26.83	19.82
	1999	94.00	94.00	82.00	80.00	86.00
Table for teacher	1996	28.57	19.15	27.73	17.07	15.32
Watcher pitcher,	1999	94.00	92.00	96.00	70.00	82.00
ladle, glasses	1996	17.46	20.21	10.92	23.17	17.12
	1999	84.00	92.00	58.00	52.00	76.00
Dustbin	1996	7.94	1.06	7.56	0.00	14.41
	1999	20.00	36.00	26.00	16.00	20.00
School bell	1996	25.40	32.98	24.37	23.17	18.02
	1999	86.00	98.00	84.00	80:00	88.00
Notice Board	1996	17.46	4.26	3.36	6.76	15.32
	1999	24.00	56.00	44.00	60.00	68.28
Play ground facility	1996	2.06	3.10	1.19	1.01	32.40
	1999	16.00	42.00	32.0	20.00	12.00
Game equipment	1996	46.67	51.43	60.00	11.90	51.35
	1999	76.00	58.00	48.00	30.00	44.00
Musical Instrument	1996	24.44	54.29	14.29	7.14	37.84
	1999	34.00	34.00	16.00	14.00	16.00
Play ground away from	1996	15.60	8.60	8.60	4.80	32.40

Facilities	Year	Bola-ngir	Dhen-kanal	Gaja-pati	Kala-handi	Raya-gada
school premises	1999	20.50	14.60	21.20	12.60	28.53
Play ground within school premises	1996	20.90	22.90	20.00	9.50	27.00
	1999	14.00	38.00	30.00	12.00	14.00
Annual medical check-up	1996	20.00	42.86	54.29	21.43	27.03
	1999	56.00	62.00	48.00	46.00	72.00
First Aid Kid	1996	11.11	5.71	8.57	0.00	32.43
	1999	16.00	20.00	22.00	78.00	28.00
Immunization facility	1996	24.44	62.86	54.21	26.19	35.14
	1999	54.00	56.00	50.00	46.00	76.00

Percentage of different essential facilities in the sample schools of the five DPEP districts, namely, Bolangir, Dhenkanal, Gajapati, Kalahandi and Rayagada (*i.e.*, over a period of three years) are presented in Table 5.2 which includes classroom requirements, health and sanitary requirements, and drinking water facilities at the basic minimum level.

A peep into the past (*i.e.*, BAS, 1996) reveals that annual medical check-up, immunization, first Aid are available in primary school respectively within the ranges of 20.00 to 54.29, 24.44 to 62.86 and 00 to 32.43 per cent schools in 1996. Although good health facilities are a premium for ensuring health care for children in a country where child mortality is high, DPEP intervention has been able to see to the realization of these goals to the extent of 46 to 72 per cent provision for health check up, 46 to 76 per cent for immunization and 16 to 78 per cent supply of first aid kit to primary schools in the above DPEP districts.

Among the essential facilities to be ensured in Primary schools, provision for safe inking water, toilet facilities, particularly, separate facilities for girls, electric connections are minimum that schools should have. The earlier study (*i.e.*, BAS, 1996) had quite depressing observations on each of these dimensions. The MAS, 1999 indicated that a marginal improvement has occurred in providing toilet facilities, the most being Gajapati (8 per cent), Kalahandi (16%), Bolangir (20%) and Dhenkanal and Rayagada (38%).

For effective teaching learning, existence of infrastructures are a must for teachers as well as students. Schools to the tune of 80 to 94 per cent have chairs/tables for teachers. However, on an average improvement has occurred in most of the essential facilities.

Table 5.3 : District-wise Percentage Distribution of Sample Teachers

District	Year	Gender		Caste			Location	
		Male	Female	SC	ST	General	Rural	Urban
Bolangir	1996	77.19	22.81	6.14	12.28	81.58	86.14	13.16
	2000	61.87	38.12	12.90	7.19	79.91	72.66	27.34
Dhenkanal	1996	75.49	24.51	6.86	11.76	81.38	87.25	12.75
	2000	61.96	38.03	4.90	7.91	87.19	68.09	31.90
Gajapati	1996	66.33	33.67	7.14	17.35	75.51	83.67	16.33
	2000	72.56	27.43	6.19	15.04	78.77	61.06	38.93
Kalahandi	1996	8100	19.00	13.33	7.78	78.89	92.00	8.00
	2000	63.38	36.62	12.67	12.67	74.66	73.14	26.05
Nayagarh	1996	79.82	20.18	5.50	11.01	83.48	81.65	18.35
	2000	63.16	36.84	4.10	5.80	90.10	78.36	21.64

Table 5.3 presents the percentage distribution of sample teachers drawn from the five DPEP districts in relation to their composition in terms of gender, rural-urban divide and caste over four years. It is apparent from the data projected in Table 5.3 that the percentage of female teachers has increased over a period of four years in all the DPEP districts except Gajapati. There is a decrease in the percentage of SC teachers in the DPEP districts like Dhenkanal, Gajapati, Kalahandi and Rayagada over the period of four years. In all the DPEP districts, excepting Kalahandi, there is a decline in the percentage of ST teachers over the period of four years. Similar, is the situation

in case of rural teachers. On the other hand, the percentage of urban teachers has increased in each DPEP district after the BAS period.

Table 5.4 : District-wise Percentage Distribution of Teachers with Respect to Professional Qualifications

Professional Qualification	Year	Bolangir		Dhenkanal		Gajapati		Kalahandi		Rayagada	
		M	F	M	F	M	F	M	F	M	F
CT	1996	94.74	68.42	82.05	68.97	89.02	83.33	90.32	77.14	92.75	73.08
	2000	90.47	79.62	78.00	69.84	87.01	77.42	87.64	88.64	75.70	81.67
B.Ed.	1996	5.26	26.32	17.95	24.14	10.98	16.67	9.68	22.86	7.75	26.92
	2000	9.53	16.66	21.00	30.16	12.98	22.58	11.23	11.36	23.36	16.67
M.Ed.	1996	00	5.26	00	6.9	00	00	00	00	00	00
	2000	00	3.72	1.07	00	00	00	1.13	00	0.94	1.66

The profile of sample teachers in terms of their professional qualifications with male-female break-up has been presented in Table 5.4. It is quite evident from the entires made in the above table that the percentage of female teachers with certificate in Elementary Education has increased over a period of four years in all the DPEP districts except Gajapati. However, there is a decrease in the percentage of female teachers with B.Ed. qualification in the DPEP districts like Bolangir, Kalahandi and Rayagada. The same trend is found among the female teachers with M.Ed. qualification in the project district like Bolangir. A phenomenon, observed in the DPEP districts of Orissa, is that greater proportion of women teachers persever have upgraded their professional qualifications over a period of four years. It may be attributed to DPEP interventions.

In view of the above results, the hypothesis (*i.e.,* 2.4.1) is partly accepted and partly rejected.

SECTION B: STUDY OF THE IMPACT OF DPEP, ORISSA ON THE RETENTION

The second objective of the investigation was to find out if there were any impact of DPEP, Orissa on the retention of the primary school children of five DPEP districts namely, Bolangir, Gajapati, Kalahandi, Dhenkanal and Rayagada. It was hypothesised that there would be positive impact of the DPEP, Orissa on the retention of the primary school children of five DPEP districts as stated above. For this, the relevant BAS (1996) data regarding enrolment and drop-out have been considered as parameters.

The structural patterns of enrolment in terms of gender, location and caste are discernible from the data presented in Table 5.5.

Removal of gender disparities in retention (also in access) is a key objective of the DPEP. The data show that in all five project districts (excepting Dhenkanal for both class III and V and Rayagada for class III), the percentage of enrolment of girls has increased. In other words, it can be said that these districts have shown the maximum gains in terms of girls' enrolment. There is a very positive development that indicates that increase in enrolment of DPEP districts like Bolangir (for class III), Gajapati and Rayagada (for class V) has been more for girls than the boys. This way it can be concluded that the DPEP objective (*i.e.,* removal of gender disparity in retention) has been to some extent, met. The innovative strategies of access and retention under DPEP have resulted in considerable increase in girls' enrolment.

It can also be observed that the percentage of urban children enrolled in the sampled schools is significantly higher than that of the urban children enrolled in the sampled schools during BAS, 1996 over six years. On the other hand, a declined trend is noticed in case of enrolment of rural children.

It is also evident from Table 5.5 that in all five DPEP districts (excepting Bolangir for class III), the percentage of enrolment of SC students has increased over six years. The percentage of ST enrolment has increased in the DPEP districts like Dhenkanal and Gajapati. On the other hand, a declined trend in ST enrolment is noticed in the DPEP districts like Bolangir, Kalahandi and Rayagada (Class III).

Table 5.5 : Percentage Distribution of Enrolment

District	Class	1996 Gender		1996 Location		1996 Caste			2002 Gender		2002 Location		2002 Caste		
		Boys	Girls	Rural	Urban	SC	ST	Gen.	Boys	Girls	Rural	Urban	SC	ST	Gen
Bolangir	III	57.40	42.60	75.80	24.20	24.28	18.81	56.92	44.79	55.21	38.54	61.54	16.67	8.33	75.00
	V	61.30	38.70	78.37	21.63	19.67	18.86	61.47	55.67	44.32	40.21	59.79	21.65	11.35	67.01
Dhenkanal	III	53.42	46.58	86.52	13.48	12.97	8.78	78.24	59.16	40.83	35.60	64.39	20.42	14.13	65.44
	V	54.43	45.57	83.29	16.71	11.27	8.61	80.12	59.75	40.24	42.68	57.32	20.12	10.36	69.51
Gajapati	III	60.64	39.36	88.06	11.94	13.49	22.97	63.09	31.39	68.60	63.95	36.05	27..32	30.23	42.44
	V	66.77	33.23	81.57	18.34	9.67	16.62	73.71	34.10	65.89	50.29	49.71	22.54	26.01	50.86
Kalahandi	III	57.40	42.60	91.54	8.46	25.81	35.13	40.05	52.40	47.59	35.80	64.19	32.75	15.72	51.22
	V	65.50	34.50	85.54	14.46	27.69	30.17	42.14	52.85	47.14	24.28	75.71	29.52	12.85	57.14
Rayagada	III	56.49	43.51	85.52	15.48	27.20	21.76	51.06	62.79	37.21	43.72	56.27	13.95	20.46	65.59
	V	66.72	33.28	83.44	16.56	10.94	19.79	69.27	49.76	50.23	40.57	59.42	14.97	40.09	44.93

Table 5.6 : Percentage Distribution of Drop-out

District	Year	Gender		Caste		Location	
		Boys	Girls	SC/ST	Gen.	Rural	Urban
Bolangir	1996	8.57	7.82	7.56	8.82	16.26	1.76
	2002	2.07	0.52	1.04	1.55	2.59	00
Dhenkanal	1996	4.75	2.56	3.04	4.27	7.12	0.19
	2002	2.81	6.48	5.08	4.22	6.48	2.82
Gajapati	1996	3.52	2.99	2.82	3.69	5.63	0.88
	2002	1.46	00	0.87	0.58	0.87	0.58
Kalahandi	1996	6.91	4.71	5.44	6.18	11.32	0.29
	2002	00	0.23	0.23	00	0.23	00
Rayagada	1996	3.84	5.52	6.48	2.88	8.28	1.08
	2002	1.66	1.18	2.84	00	2.36	0.47

Table 5.6 displays the gender-wise, location wise, and caste-wise distribution of drop-outs over a period of six years in the five DPEP districts. The data indicate that in all DPEP districts (excepting Dhenkanal), the incidence of girls drop-out has decreased, similar is the situation in case of SC/ST drop-out. A declined trend has also been observed in case of rural dropouts in all DPEP districts. Thus, it can be concluded that the percentage of retention has been increased over six years.

In view of the above results, the hypothesis (*i.e.*, 2.4.2) was partly accepted and partly rejected.

SECTION C: ASSESSMENT AND COMPARISON OF LEARNERS' ACHIEVEMENT ON BASELINE ASSESSMENT STUDY (BAS)

The baseline assessment study (BAS) was initially conducted in five DPEP districts of Orissa, namely, Bolangir, Dhenkanal, Gajapati, Kalahandi and Rayagada in 1996. The purpose of the study was to study the primary level educational status of the proposed districts prior to implementation of the project interventions. The results particularly relating to learners achievement can be used to examine the impact of project interventions from time to time particularly at the end of the project period.

With this perspective in view, tests of achievement to assess the levels of attainment in language and mathematics of the students of class V and in literacy and numeracy of class II students and drop-outs were administered by the Directorate, T.E. and S.C.E.R.T., Orissa, Bhubaneswar. The sample for the study comprised 513 teachers, 1801 class V students, 2125 class II students and 358 drop-outs.

The data collected under the baseline assessment studies have been re-analysed for the purposes of present investigation. However, an attempt is made here only to re-analyse the performance of the learners of class II in literacy (*i.e.*, language) and numeracy in 'terms of gender, location and caste'. The results are presented in Table 5.7 through Table 5.13.

Table 5.7 : Achievement of Class II Students in Language (Oriya) and Numeracy

Districts	N.	Maximum marks	Achievement in language		Achievement in numeracy	
			M	SD	M	SD
Bolangir	431	20	10.07	3.72	6.91	3.96
Dhenkanal	523	20	13.77	3.53	9.45	4.18
Gajapati	332	20	14.50	3.33	9.23	4.62
Kalahandi	398	20	8.91	4.16	5.93	5.04
Rayagada	441	20	13.43	3.75	8.21	4.90

Table 5.7 indicates that the average performance of the class II students of Gajapati district in language (M = 14.5) was higher than their counterparts in the other DPEP districts. It was followed by Dhenkanal (M = 13.77) and Rayagada (M = 14.33). So far as their performance in language was concerned the students from Bolangir district and Kalahandi district were located at the lowest end of the continuum.

The comparison of average performance of students of class II in numeracy across the DPEP districts revealed that the over all performance of students was abysmally low. The class II students of Dhenkanal district have the highest average score of 9.45 and those of Kalahandi district had the mean score of 5.93 in numeracy test which is minimum among the five districts.

It can also be seen (vide Table 5.7) that the students of class II have performed better in language as compared to numeracy. It is evident from higher mean performance scores on language than numeracy in all the five DPEP districts. The pattern of variation in the performance of students, across the districts in language was almost the same as in numeracy of all the districts, the performance of students of class II from Kalahandi and Bolangir was at the lowest ebb.

Gender-wise achievement of students of class II in language (*i.e.*, scores on letter reading and word reading) in terms of the mean and SD of scores in respect of all five districts are presented in Table 5.8.

Table 5.8 : Gender-wise Achievement of Class II Students in Language

Areas of Language	Districts	Boys		Girls		
		M	SD	M	SD	
Letter Reading	Bolangir	5.73	3.53	4.95	3.56	*
	Dhenkanal	7.47	3.04	7.12	3.38	
	Gajapati	7.57	2.97	7.80	3.14	
	Kalahandi	5.05	4.04	5.33	3.98	
	Rayagada	6.84	3.53	6.52	4.01	
Word Reading	Bolangir	5.14	3.93	4.21	3.83	*
	Dhenkanal	6.45	3.83	6.32	3.92	
	Gajapati	6.73	3.56	7.05	3.76	
	Kalahandi	3.79	4.26	3.69	4.18	
	Rayagada	6.28	3.91	5.99	4.26	

*Difference is significant.

The scores on the two components of the language tests *i.e.*, on Letter Reading and Word Reading split on gender basis (c.f. Table 5.8) demonstrates over all superior performance on Letter Reading irrespective of gender difference. The gender difference on both the components of the test is not significant for any district except in Bolangir district. The hypothesis *i.e.,* 2.4.3 (1) is partly accepted and partly rejected.

Table 5.9 shows mean and S.D. of scores on Letter Reading and Word Reading of pupils in the rural and urban schools. The mean scores on both components are higher for pupils reading in urban schools, urban pupils demonstrating significantly better performance in all the districts. Students of urban schools of Dhenkanal have the highest average in both the components with least variance while those in the rural schools of Kalahandi have the lowest average with maximum variance among the ten groups. Hence the hypothesis 2.4.3 (II) is retained.

Table 5.9 : Achievement of Class II Students in Language (Location-wise)

Areas of Language	Districts	Rural		Urban		
		M	SD	M	SD	
Letter Reading	Bolangir	5.01	3.45	7.15	3.64	*
	Dhenkanal	7.09	3.27	9.25	1.40	*
	Gajapati.	7.40	3.11	9.02	2.11	*
	Kalahandi	5.02	3.96	6.76	4.28	*
	Rayagada	6.53	3.74	7.97	3.34	*
Word Reading	Bolangir	4.38	3.75	6.33	4.27	*
	Dhenkanal	6.12	3.86	9.16	2.10	*
	Gajapati	5.50	3.72	8.73	2.37	*
	Kalahandi	3.63	4.20	5.10	4.41	*
	Rayagada	5.96	4.02	6.78	3.94	*

*Difference is significant.

The caste-wise achievement of the student of Class II in language (*i.e.,* Letter Reading and Word Reading) in term of Mean and S.D. of Scores for the above five districts have been presented in Table 5.10.

Table 5.10 : Achievement of Class II Students in Language (Caste-wise)

Areas of Language	Districts	SC/ST		Others/NSC/ST		
		M	SD	M	SD	
Letter Reading	Bolangir	5.18	3.44	5.48	3.64	
	Dhenkanal	6.36	3.59	7.60	3.00	*
	Gajapati	6.81	3.34	8.18	2.68	*
	Kalahandi	4.64	4.04	6.04	3.80	*
	Rayagada	6.31	3.72	7.21	3.65	*
Word Reading	Bolangir	4.77	3.71	4.67	4.03	
	Dhenkanal	5.37	4.12	6.77	3.68	*
	Gajapati	5.82	4.05	7.49	3.18	*
	Kalahandi	3.14	4.05	4.78	4.31	*
	Rayagada	5.67	4.05	6.78	3.94	*

* Difference is significant.

A close look at Table 5.10 revealed that SC/ST children having highest mean scores in Letter Reading and Word Reading are in Gajapati district and die lowest in Kalahandi district. It is evident from the table that in all the districts barring Bolangir, the inter group difference between SC/ST and other groups are significant. It implies that children belonging to SC and ST groups performed at a significantly lower level than their counterpart in the general caste category. The hypothesis *i.e.,* 2.4.3. (iii) is accepted.

Gender-wise achievement of students of Class II in numeracy (*i.e.,* Number Recognition and Addition and Subtraction) in terms of the mean and S.D. of scores in respect of all five districts are presented in Table 5.11.

In gender-wise distribution of means and standard deviations as evidenced in Table 5.11, it is seen that the mean of scores on numeracy of boys are more than that of girls. But only on difference in addition and subtraction components of the numeracy test is significant in Bolangir district. In no other districts the gender difference was conspicuously significant.

Hence, the hypothesis 2.4.4. (1) is partly accepted and partly rejected.

Table 5.11 : Gender-wise Achievement of Class II Students in Numeracy

Areas	Districts	Boys		Girls		Total		
		M	SD	M	SD	M	SD	
Number	Bolangir	3.64	1.68	3.29	1.76	3.48	1.73	
Recognition	Dhenkanal	4.65	1.54	4.45	1.75	4.56	1.63	
	Gajapati	4.27	1.85	4.12	1.90	4.22	1.87	
	Kalahandi	3.20	2.25	3.09	2.19	3.16	2.23	
	Rayagada	4.11	2.01	4.08	2.10	4.10	2.04	
Addition and	Bolangir	3.82	2.83	2.97	2.75	3.42	2.82	*
subtraction	Dhenkanal	5.09	2.93	4.61	3.00	4.88	2.97	
	Gajapati	3.17	2.81	2.70	3.38	3.00	3.13	
	Kalahandi	2.77	3.27	2.75	3.14	2.76	3.22	
	Rayagada	4.29	3.16	3.82	3.35	4.12	3.23	

* Difference is significant.

In the location wise distribution of the means (cf. Table 5.12), the rural-urban divide is quite conspicuous. Not only the urban school students have higher mean scores in both the components of numeracy test (*i.e.,* number recognition and addition and subtraction) but also the rural-urban differences are significant in all districts except for Rayagada in the number recognition component. Hence the hypothesis 2.4.4 (ii) is accepted.

The group means and S.D. Calculated for the two social groups *i.e.,* SC/ST and other general presented in Table 5.13 revealed that average performance of SC/ST students in numeracy is lower than that of the students belonging to general castes as observed in all the districts. But the significant difference in both number recognition and addition and subtraction could only be observable in Gajapati district. Hence, the hypothesis 2.4.4. (iii) is partially rejected.

Table 5.12 : Achievement of Class II Students in Numeracy (Location-wise)

Areas	Districts	Rural		Urban		
		M	SD	M	SD	
Number	Bolangir	3.30	1.67	4.34	1.74	*
Recognition	Dhenkanal	4.42	1.66	5.73	0.67	*
	Gajapati	3.96	1.89	5.59	0.86	*
	Kalahandi	3.07	2.19	4.15	2.38	*
	Rayagada	3.92	2.05	4.07	2.09	
Addition and	Bolangir	3.31	2.70	3.98	3.34	*
subtraction	Dhenkanal	4.66	2.97	6.78	2.20	*
	Gajapati	4.09	5.10	7.88	1.78	*
	Kalahandi	2.64	3.14	4.12	3.78	*
	Rayagada	3.94	3.18	5.18	1.63	*

* Difference is significant.

Table 5.13 : Achievement of Class II Students in Numeracy (Caste-wise)

Areas	Districts	SC/ST		Others		
		M	SD	M	SD	
Number	Bolangir	3.33	1.70	3.57	1.74	
Recognition	Dhenkanal	4.18	1.77	4.68	1.57	
	Gajapati	3.73	1.83	4.52	1.83	*
	Kalahandi	2.98	2.17	3.46	2.29	
	Rayagada	3.84	2.11	4.40	1.91	
Addition and	Bolangir	3.60	2.75	3.31	2.87	
substraction	Dhenkanal	4.32	3.60	5.06	2.02	
	Gajapati	4.07	0.20	5.50	2.08	*
	Kalahandi	2.44	3.11	3.30	3.34	
	Rayagada	3.62	3.24	4.71	3.13	

* Difference significant.

SECTION D: ASSESSMENT AND COMPARISON OF LEARNERS' ACHIEVEMENT ON MID-TERM ASSESSMENT SURVEY (MAS)

As per the stipulation of the World Bank Report (1994), the assessment studies are to be conducted during the third and sixth year of the project. The Mid-Term Assessment Survey (MAS) serves as a mid-way check point to examine if the planned intervention strategies are moving in the right direction resulting in positive results.

The MAS have been conducted in the above five DPEP districts in 1999. The sample for the study comprised 728 teachers, 2803 class IV students and 2739 class I students. The data collected under the MAS have been reanalysed for the purposes of present investigation. The analysis has been restricted only to the performance of the students of class IV, both in language and mathematics and the results have been presented in Table 5.14 through Table 5.25.

Gender-wise and Area-wise achievement of class IV students in language in terms of mean and means of the percentages scores for all the five districts have been presented in Table 5.14.

Table 5.14 presents the mean percentage achievement in language for the sub-groups generated in terms of gender and area. The CR values are also indicated for validations of the inter group differences wherever this was found.

The data failed to yield significant gender differences in language in rural group and total group students. However, in case of urban sample the superiority of girls over boys was seen in case of Gajapati, Kalahandi and Rayagada district which are statistically significant.

As regards rural-urban divide in respect of boys, girls and total, the data indicated that rural girls invariably scored less in language than their urban counterparts. Boys were divided in their rural-urban divide superiority. The rural total group of students scored less in two districts than urban ones. In one district it was reverse, and in the remaining two no such differences were observed. Hence, the hypothesis 2.4.5 (I) is partly accepted and partly rejected.

Table 5.14 : Gender-wise and Area-wise Achievement of Class IV Students in Language (Oriya)

District	Gender	Rural			Urban			Total			CR Value (R-U)
		N	Mean %	SD	N	Mean %	SD	N	Mean %	SD	
Bolangir	Boys	197	43.95	11.9	92	46.19	15.95	289	44.66	13.32	1.2
	Girls	180	43	12.26	73	43.85	15.68	253	43.24	13.34	0.41
	Total	377	43.49	12.07	165	45.16	15.83	542	44.00	13.33	1.2
	CR Value		0.76			0.94			1.23		
Dhenkanal	Boys	307	62.96	8.89	135	65.15	9.93	442	63.63	9..22	2.19 *
	Girls	249	62.71	9.45	117	66.76	8.75	366	64.01	9.24	401 **
	Total	556	62.85	9.15	252	65.90	9.40	808	63.80	9.23	4.29 **
	CR.Value		0.31			1.36			0.57		
Gajapati	Boys	189	63.03	11.25	75	60.38	13.73	264	62.27	12.01	1.48
	Girls	112	60.71	13.32	74	64.47	11.47	186	62.21	12.62	2.05 *
	Total	301	62.16	12.06	149	62.41	12.66	450	62.25	12.26	0.19
	CR Value		1.54			1.97*			0.05		

Kalahandi	Boys	172	47.42	11.87	51	36.97	10.38	223	45.03	11.54	6.10 **
	Girls	162	47.14	13.02	56	41.04	10.54	218	45.57	12.43	3.50 **
	Total	334	47.28	12.44	107	39.10	10.47	441	45.3	11.99	6.71 **
	CR Value		0.2			2.01*			0.47		
Rayagada	Boys	266	51.94	12.60	53	53.39	11.41	319	52.18	12.41	0.82
	Girls	176	49.59	12.30	67	63.34	8.65	243	53.38	11.41	9.78 **
	Total	442	51.01	12.48	120	58.95	9.96	562	52.70	11.99	7.31 **
	CR Value		1.95			5.26**			1.18		

*p<.05, **p<.01

Table 5.15 presents data on language achievement in terms of mean percentages for the boys and girls of class IV against their SC/ST and other group membership. The inter group CR values are also mentioned.

It is evident from Table 5.15 that in case of SC, the gender specific differences is not very clear in response to language achievement across districts when compared with others. No inter group difference was seen except for the district of Dhenkanal, for SC girls, where they were found to be significantly below others including OBC. Performance of SC Boys were significantly inferior to others in two districts (Dhenkanal and Rayagada). These isolated cases have no relevance for generalization on inter group caste differences rather one would be fair enough to conclude that caste differences in case of language acquisition does not exist for boys, girls and total groups, so far as SC and others are concerned.

As regards ST vs. others comparison the results are not in any way different. ST girls in three districts were found significantly scoring lower than others in total language scores. So also the ST total vs. others. Only in one district ST Boys scored significantly less than others. In all other cases inter-group differences were not significant.

The results are not very conclusive on language acquisition as regards differential achievement. Rather, it can be stated that by and large, barring the district of Dhenkanal, SC/ST students irrespective of gender, performed at the same level as others including OBC in language achievement tests. The Upper Level performance is not quite high. Hence the hypothesis *i.e.*, 2.4.5 (ii) is partially accepted and partially rejected.

Language Achievement Scores in respect of class IV students belonging to SC, ST and other category and coming from rural and urban area of five districts included in the study are presented in Table 5.16 along with CR values to testify the intergroup differences, if any.

The data presented in Table 5.16 indicate that both rural and urban SC students exhibit significantly inferior performance compared to others but this has occurred in two out of five districts. SC in general performed as well as others which

Table 5.15 : Gender-wise and Caste-wise Achievement of Class IV Students in Language

District	Gender	SC			ST			Others			Total			Cr Value (SC: others)	CR Value (ST: others)
		N	Mean%	SD	N	Mean%	SD	N	Mean %	SD	N	Mean%	SD		
Bolangir	Boys	62	47.35	12.65	50	43.08	12.51	177	44.17	13.73	289	44.66	13.3	1.66	0.53
	Girls	46	45.52	15.14	37	39.34	11.4	170	43.47	13.12	253	43.24	13.28	0.83	1.94
	Total	108	46.57	13.76	87	41.49	12.05	347	43.83	13.44	542	44.00	13.29	1.81	1.58
Dhenkanal	Boys	71	60.3	8.35	58	58.47	9.23	313	65.34	9.17	442	63.63	9.05	4.51 **	5.21 **
	Girls	62	61.15	9.47	26	61.64	7.22	278	64.87	9.39	366	64.01	9.27	2.79 **	2.11 *
	Total	133	60.69	8.89	84	59.45	8.66	591	65.12	9.27	808	63.8	9.15	5.14 **	5.56 **
Gajapati	Boys	110	63.28	11.71	63	59.84	10.31	91	62.74	13.36	264	62.27	12	0.3	1.52
	Girls	62	61.15	13.66	45	61.26	12.79	79	63.58	11.73	186	62.21	12.66	1.11	0.99
	Total	172	62.51	12.44	108	60.43	11.41	170	63.13	12.63	450	62.25	12.27	0.45	1.84
Kalahandi	Boys	69	45.36	10.66	41	43.31	10.25	113	45.46	13.17	223	45.03	11.93	0.05	1.06
	Girls	62	45.5	10.59	48	40.77	10.42	108	47.75	14.1	218	45.57	12.42	1.17	3.44 **
	Total	131	45.43	10.63	89	41.94	10.34	221	46.58	13.63	441	45.3	12.18	0.88	3.24 **
	Boys	68	49.85	9.5	95	52.34	12.39	156	53.11	13.44	319	52.18	12.38	2.06 *	2.46
Rayagada	Girls	60	53.23	11.53	58	50.73	11.79	125	54.68	12.58	243	53.38	12.14	0.77	2.06 *
	Total	128	51.43	10.5	153	51.73	12.16	281	53.81	13.07	562	52.7	12.28	1.95	1.65

*P<.05, **P<.01.

Table 5.16 : Area-wise and Caste-wise Achievement of Class IV Students in Language

District	Area	SC N	SC Mean%	SC SD	ST N	ST Mean%	ST SD	Others N	Others Mean %	Others SD	Total N	Total Mean%	Total SD	Cr Value (SC: others)	CR Value (ST: others)
Bolangir	Rural	81	49.31	12.95	68	40.14	11.18	228	42.43	11.67	377	43.49	11.87	4.21 **	1.46
	Urban	27	38.35	14.57	19	46.31	14.49	119	46.51	16.14	165	45.16	15.71	2.57 *	0.05
	Total	108	46.57	13.37	87	41.49	11.98	347	43.83	13.37	542	44	13.16	1.86	1.58
Dhenkanal	Rural	89	60.28	8.73	81	59.77	8.72	386	64.09	9.19	556	62.85	9.05	3.67 **	4.02 **
	Urban	44	61.52	9.2	3	50.95	6.34	205	67.05	9.28	252	65.9	9.23	3.61 **	4.33 **
	Total	133	60.69	8.89	84	59.45	8.64	591	65.12	9.22	808	63.8	9.11	5.15 **	5.57 **
Gajapati	Rural	121	62.93	13.29	98	60.07	11.49	82	63.53	10.68	301	62.16	12.04	0.35	2.09 *
	Urban	51	61.51	10.22	10	64.00	10.42	88	62.75	14.2	149	62.41	12.73	0.59	0.34
	Total	172	62.51	12.46	108	60.43	11.39	170	63.13	12.63	450	62.25	12.27	0.45	1.84
Kalahandi	Rural	96	47.52	10.93	82	42.64	10.5	156	49.57	13.84	334	47.28	12.28	1.30	4.32 **
	Urban	35	39.67	8.51	7	33.67	6.43	65	39.38	11.77	107	39.1	10.51	0.14	201 *
	Total	131	45.43	10.34	89	41.94	10.24	221	46.58	13.26	441	45.3	11.88	0.90	3.30 **
Rayagada	Rural	88	48.36	10.5	139	51.11	12.44	215	52.03	13.21	442	51.01	12.47	2.55 *	0.66
	Urban	40	58.21	9.06	14	57.95	7.96	66	59.61	11.77	120	58.95	10.54	0.68	0.64
	Total	128	51.43	10.07	153	51.73	12.1	281	53.81	12.88	562	52.7	12.08	2.01 *	1.66

$^*p<.05$, $^{**}p<.01$

includes OBC in language achievement with minor variations in districts.

Results in two districts concerning ST groups of students are significantly different for rural ST vs. Urban ST, and total when compared with that of others (Dhenkanal and Kalahandi). In these districts both rural and Urban as well as the total group of ST students are significantly lower in Language achievement than their respective others group counterparts. So the hypothesis is partially accepted and partially rejected.

Gender-wise and Area-wise achievement of class IV students in Mathematics in terms of mean and means of the percentages scores for all the five districts have been presented in Table 5.17.

The mean percentage of Mathematics achievement scores of students reading in Class IV are presented in Table 5.17 separately for the four sub-groups generated by gender (Boys and Girls) and area (rural and urban) along with the total group. The inter group differences using mean achievement scores were tested by using CRs. The CR values are given in Table 5.17.

From the pool of data in Table 5.17, the following generalisation could be drawn with certainty. Gender-wise differences did occur in case of both rural and urban sample and their total in two of five districts. In each case, however, the boys scored higher in Mathematics than did girls. One exception however, is seen *i.e.,* in case of Rayagada district Urban girls and total girls (Rural + Urban) group scored higher than their counterpart boys.

Gender specific rural urban differences in Mathematics are not very clear cut and the trend of differences are mixed up Wherever difference did occur in case of some districts the rural boys are inferior to urban boys (Dhenkanal); in others the reverse is true *i.e.,* (Bolangir and Kalahandi) whereas there is no such rural urban girls comparison has yielded no conclusive inference. Hence, both can be constructed as equal in Mathematics achievement at class IV level. The performance level has hardly crossed the 50 per cent limit and at the lower end it is 29 per cent which is of course not encouraging in terms

Table 5.17 : Gender-wise and Area-wise Achievement of Class IV Students in Mathematics

District	Gender	Rural			Urban			Total			CR Value (R-U)
		N	Mean %	SD	N	Mean %	SD	N	Mean %	SD	
Bolangir	Boys	197	37.34	7.01	92	35.43	6.99	289	36.73	7.00	2.16 *
	Girls	180	31.08	7.16	73	30.27	5.61	253	30.84	6.75	0.95
	Total	377	34.35	7.08	165	33.15	6.41	542	33.98	6.88	1.94
	CR Value		8.57**			5.26**			9.95**		
Dhenkanal	Boys	307	56.07	8.70	135	59.01	8.06	442	56.97	8.51	3.44 **
	Girls	249	52.01	7.87	117	52.26	7.77	366	52.09	7.84	0.28
	Total	556	54.25	8.34	252	55.88	7.93	808	54.76	8.22	2.65 **
	CR Value		5.76**			6.76**			8.46'*		
Gajapati	Boys	189	53.09	7.13	75	54.33	6.70	264	53.44	7.01	1.32
	Girls	112	52.92	6.97	74	52.33	7.99	186	52.68	7.39	0.52
	Total	301	53.03	7.07	149	53.33	7.37	450	53.13	7.17	0.42
	CR Value		0.2			1.65			1.09		

Kalahandi	Boys	172	34.24	7.10	51	29.8	5.00	223	33.22	6.68	5.01	**
	Girls	162	33.79	8.17	56	28.70	5.80	218	32.48	7.63	5.05	**
	Total	334	34.02	7.64	107	29.22	5.43	441	32.86	7.17	7.14	**
	CR Value		0.53			1.05			1.08			
Rayagada	Boys	266	38.87	7.91	53	39.29	6.93	319	38.94	7.75	0.39	
	Girls	176	39.87	7.48	67	48.54	6	243	42.26	7.10	9.38	**
	Total	442	39.27	7.74	120	44.45	6.42	562	40.37	7.48	7.49	**
	CR Value		1.34			7.70**			5.27**			

*p<.05, **p<.01.

of the inputs that has gone into the system. Hence, hypothesis *i.e.,* 2.4.6 (i) is partly accepted and partly rejected.

Table 5.18 presents the mean percentage achievement scores in mathematics for students of class IV for SC, ST, other including OBC and gender groups (Boys and Girls) separately along with inter group difference indicator CR values.

The results presented in Table 5.18 show mixed finding. In three districts SC-boys have scored less than boys belonging to others category, whereas in the remaining two (Gajapati and Rayagada) their scores are higher than others. In all these cases the differences are statistically significant. As regards SC-girls vs, others (girls) only in case one district, SC-girls scored high (Gajapati) and in Dhenkanal and Kalahandi SC girls were significantly low achievers than girls belonging to other castes. In the remaining two districts there is no difference.

As regards SC students in general, the results are same as that of SC boys. Hence, neither gender clubbed difference within SC nor gender specific difference between SC and others could be established clearly.

On the other hand, when ST boys/ST girls, ST total groups were compared respectively with boys, girls, total belonging to other caste including OBCs the ST caste groups did score significantly low in Mathematics achievement test than the comparison groups. In other words ST boys, ST girls, ST in general are significantly poor performers than others including OBCs.

Mathematics achievement scores in terms of Mean percentages have been given in Table 5.19 for the SC, ST and other caste against the area of residence (Rural, Urban) separately.

It can be seen from Table 5.19 that ST students whether they come from rural or urban background and/or mixed more often are significantly low scorers in Mathematics Achievement Tests than their respective counterparts in others including OBCs.

In case of SC vs. others comparison on the basis of rural urban divide, the results are equivocal in the sense that Rural

Table 5.18 : Gender-wise and Caste-wise Achievement of Class IV Students in Mathematics

District	Gender	SC N	SC Mean%	SC SD	ST N	ST Mean%	ST SD	Others N	Others Mean %	Others SD	Total N	Total Mean%	Total SD	Cr Value (SC: others)	CR Value (ST: others)
Bolangir	Boys	62	34.27	7.29	50	33.70	6.57	177	38.46	6.94	289	36.73	6.95	3.93 **	4.46 **
	Girls	46	32.55	6.75	37	24.59	6.70	170	31.75	6.64	253	30.84	6.67	0.71 *	5.89 **
	Total	108	33.54	7.07	87	29.82	6.63	347	35.17	6.80	542	33.98	6.82	2.11 *	6.69 **
Dhenkanal	Boys	71	50.31	8.92	58	47.97	7.90	313	60.15	8.22	442	56.97	8.29	8.50 **	10.71 **
	Girls	62	47.01	7.94	26	49.51	7.18	278	53.47	7.79	366	52.09	7.78	5.80 **	2.66 **
	Total	133	48.77	8.48	84	48.45	7.68	591	57.00	8.02	808	54.76	8.06	10.21 **	9.49 **
Gajapari	Boys	110	56.61	7.03	63	51.54	6.93	91	50.93	6.82	264	53.44	6.93	5.79 **	0.54
	Girls	62	55.08	8.14	45	51.94	7.27	79	51.23	6.75	186	52.68	7.36	2.99 **	0.53
	Total	172	56.06	7.45	108	51.71	7.07	170	51.07	6.79	450	53.13	7.11	6.47 **	0.74

*p<.05, **p<.01

Table 5.19 : Area-wise and Caste-wise Achievement of Class IV Students in Mathematics

District	Area	SC			ST			Others			Total			Cr Value (SC: others)	CR Value (ST: others)
		N	Mean%	SD	N	Mean%	SD	N	Mean %	SD	N	Mean%	SD		
Bolangir	Rural	81	36.26	7.22	68	29.15	6.68	228	35.23	7.22	377	34.35	7.12	1.10	6.46 **
	Urban	27	25.37	5.46	19	32.23	7.43	119	35.06	6.33	165	33.15	6.34	8.07 **	1.57
	Total	108	33.54	6.82	87	29.82	6.85	347	35.17	6.93	542	33.98	6.89	2.16 *	6.49 **
Dhenkanal	Rural	89	48.84	8.92	81	48.48	7.78	386	56.71	8.18	556	54.25	8.25	7.61 **	8.57 **
	Urban	44	48.63	7.59	3	47.50	4.55	205	57.56	8.02	252	55.88	7.92	7.00 **	3.74 **
	Total	133	48.77	8.51	84	48.45	7.69	591	57.00	8.13	808	54.76	8.15	10.16 **	9.47 **
Gajapati	Rural	121	55.26	7.02	98	52.19	7.13	82	50.73	6.92	301	53.03	7.03	4.55 **	1.39
	Urban	51	57.94	8.34	47.00	47	6.16	88	51.39	6.66	149	53.33	7.25	4.79 **	2.11 *
	Total	172	56.06	7.44	108	51.71	7.04	170	51.07	6.79	450	53.13	7.10	6.48 **	0.74
Kalahandi	Rural	96	31.64	6.53	82	30.36	7.65	156	37.41	8.02	334	34.02	7.53	6.24 **	6.64 **
	Urban	35	28.42	5.75	7	28.92	4.89	65	29.69	5.31	107	29.22	5.43	1.07	0.38
	Total	131	30.78	6.33	89	30.25	7.47	221	35.14	7.33	441	32.86	7.08	5.88 **	5.24 **
Rayagada	Rural	88	42.04	7.26	139	37.14	8.49	215	39.51	7.35	442	39.27	7.71	2.74 **	2.70 **
	Urban	40	44.37	5.40	14	40.53	7.92	66	45.34	7.04	120	44.45	6.65	0.79	2.10 *
	Total	128	42.77	6.74	153	37.45	8.44	281	40.88	7.28	562	40.37	7.50	2.56 *	4.23 **

*p<.05, **p<.01.

SC are superior to others in the districts of Gajapati and Rayagada, whereas in Dhenkanal and Kalahandi they are significantly low compared to others in Mathematics achievement.

The urban SC in two districts (Bolangir and Dhenkanal) have scored significantly low in achievement (Mathematics) than Urban others. In the district of Gajapati, however, urban SC is superior to urban others. When rural and urban groups are combined a more clear picture emerged *i.e.,* SC in general are significantly inferior to others including OBC in mathematics achievement. Moreover, direction of group difference in SC vs. others has become district specific.

In view of the above results the hypothesis *i.e.,* 2.4.6 (ii) is partly accepted and partly rejected.

Further an attempt has been made to findout the achievement differences in regard to area, gender and caste reflected on MAS in 1999. A detailed account of area-wise differences in achievement both in language and Mathematics in respect of class IV followed by gender-wise and then caste-wise analysis has been presented below:

Table 5.20 presents mean percentage of achievement in language for the urban and rural areas in each district for class IV students in MAS.

Table 5.20 : Area-wise Comparison of Achievement Differences of Class IV Students' Performance in Language Exhibited on the Mid-Term Assessment Tests

District	Urban			Rural			CR values	
	N	Mean%,	SD	N	Mean %	SD	(U:R)	
Bolangir	30	33.84	13.83	71	44.83	13.34	3.68	**
Dhenkanal	48	60.91	14.54	107	56.14	16.46	1.81	
Gajapati	35	62.14	18.30	50	48.3	15.86	3.62	**
Kalahandi	14	38.52	9.94	88	42.99	11.68	1.52	
Rayagada	27	44.26	16.78	76	38.95	19.65	1.34	

* P < .05, **P< 0.1.

Table 5.20 displays that in almost three districts (Dhenkanal, Kalahandi and Rayagada) DPEP interventions have resulted in bringing the gaps between rural-urban divide. The CR-values are all insignificant.

Only in one district (Gajapati) urban students achieved more in language than rural students while the rural students achieved more in language than the urban students in case of Bolangir district.

The gender-wise mean percentage of achievement in language on MAS are presented in Table 5.21 alongwith the CR values indicating significance of intergroup variations.

Table 5.21 : Gender-wise Comparison of Achievement Differences of Class IV Students' Performance in Language Exhibited on the Mid-Term Assessment Tests

District	Boys			Girls			CR values
	N	Mean%,	SD	N	Mean %	SD	(U:R)
Bolangir	51	42.88	14.93	50	40.23	13.18	0.94 ns
Dhenkanal	80	59.64	15.3	75	55.46	16.51	1.63 ns
Gajapati	56	53.72	18.00	29	54.55	17.53	0.20 ns
Kalahandi	43	44.26	12.57	59	41.00	10.56	1.38 ns
Rayagada	47	38.27	21.15	56	42.09	16.93	0.99 ns

P < .05, **P < .01 ns : Not Significant.

The results reveal certain trends of establishing boys' superiority in three districts (Bolangir, Dhenkanal and Kalahandi) and girls superiority in two districts but these differences when examined in terms of CR values, failed to reach the significance level. Hence, it would be safe to say that gender divide did not reflect in achievement differences in language for class IV students which is supportive of achieving the goals of DPEP intervention in a way.

Mean percentage in language achievement for SC, ST and other students studying in class IV are given in Table 5.22. The inter group differences have also been mentioned to signify whether such differences are real and not due to chance.

Table 5.22 : Caste-wise Comparison of Achievement Differences of Class IV Students' Performance in Language Exhibited on the Mid-Term Assessment Tests

District	SC			ST			Other			CR Values (SC: others)	CR Values (ST: others)
	N	Mean%	SD	N	Mean%	SD	N	Mean %	SD		
Bolangir	23	43.68	14.43	24	40.87	14.21	54	40.98	13.91	0.76	0.03
Dhenkanal	24	59.62	19.59	21	47.27	10.39	110	59.15	22.74	0.10	3.78 **
Gajapati	42	47.44	16.30	13	58.79	18.54	30	61.11	26.35	2.51 *	0.32
Kalahandi	36	41.56	10.08	13	35.98	11.18	53	44.49	12.68	1.21	2.39 *
Rayagada	23	42.44	12.56	33	44.48	19.42	47	36.42	21.29	1.48	1.75

p<.05 *p<.01.

Table 5.22 revealed that in Gajapati district only SC students were significantly inferior in language to others including OBC. For all other districts the SC—other divide did not exist. Superiority of others over ST in language achievement is significantly observed in case of two districts (Dhenkanal and Kalahandi) and in the remaining three districts there was no difference. These findings thus substantiate efficacy of DPEP interventions in bridging the gap as an innovative step towards UEE.

The urban-rural divide mean percentage, achievement scores are given in Table 5.23 in respect of Mathematics achievement in MAS. The intergroup, difference (CR values) are mentioned along with the data.

Table 5.23 : Area-wise Comparison of Achievement Differences of Class IV Students' Performance in Mathematics Exhibited on the Mid-Term Assessment Tests

District	Urban			Rural			CR values (U:R)	
	N	Mean%,	SD	N	Mean %	SD		
Bolangir	30	26.33	4.95	71	43.06	9.48	11.58	**
Dhenkanal	48	65.36	11.97	107	49.67	6.51	8.53	**
Gajapati	35	54.21	9.01	50	42.25	7.74	6.38	**
Kalahandi	14	42.85	6.89	88	35.05	4.9	4.07	**
Rayagada	27	33.05	7.25	76	35.23	9.28	1.23	

*P <. 05, **P < .01.

The statistical analysis (vide Table 5.23) revealed that urban students in class IV had significantly higher achievement scores on Mathematics than the rural students in three out of five districts (Gajapati, Dhenkanal and Kalahandi). In one district (Bolangir), the rural students were significantly better than urban students and equality was established in the other districts. Hence, with increase in educational level, the urban-rural divide is becoming imperative.

The mean percentage of mathematics achievement scores for Boys and Girls are presented in Table 5.24 for each districts separately along with their CR-values signifying inter-group differences, if any.

Table 5.24 : Gender-wise Comparison of Achievement Differences of Class IV Students' Performance in Mathematics Exhibited on the Mid-Term Assessment Tests

District	Boys			Girls			CR values (B : G)	
	N	Mean%,	SD	N	Mean %	SD		
Bolangir	51	39.01	85	50	37.15	9.35	1.05	
Dhenkanal	80	57.12	9.5	75	51.76	8.43	3.72	**
Gajapati	56	46.16	7.55	29	49.13	10.32	1.37	
Kalahandi	43	36.86	5.47	59	35.59	5.21	1.17	
Rayagada	47	31.96	10.09	56	36.91	7.42	2.78	**

* P <.05, **T < .01.

A close perusal of Table 5.24 indicates that in three districts (Bolangir, Gajapati and Kalahandi) gender difference in Mathematics did not exist as CRs are insignificant. In the district of Dhenkanal boys wore significantly superior to girls and in Rayagada district reverse was true. The CRs being significant in both cases it can be said to be real. However, the magnitude of difference is maximum five.

The mean percentage scores in mathematics for class IV students belonging to SC, ST and others are presented in Table 5.25. The CR values are mentioned to indicate the significance level of differences between comparison groups SC vs. others; and ST vs. others.

An examination of the data presented in Table 5.25 shows that in two of three districts (Bolangir and Dhenkanal), SC students significantly did better in mathematics achievement tests than others but in Gajapati district others did better than SC students.

In the remaining two other districts, namely Kalahandi and Rayagada there was no significant difference in achievement in Mathematics in MAS. In case of STs in two out of three districts (Bolangir and Rayagada) STs were superior to others

Table 5.25 : Caste-wise Comparison of Achievement Differences of Class IV Students' Performance in Mathematics Exhibited on the Mid-Term Assessment Tests

District	SC			ST			Other			CR Values	CR Values
	N	Mean%	SD	N	Mean%	SD	N	Mean %	SD	(SC: others)	(ST: others)
Bolangir	23	42.39	11.53	24	41.14	9.13	54	34.90	7.22	2.88 **	2.96 **
Dhenkanal	24	62.91	11.41	21	43.45	6.07	110	54.81	12.34	3.10 **	6.41 **
Gajapati	42	41.36	7.51	13	49.03	8.33	30	54.50	12.27	5.20 **	1.69
Kalahandi	36	35.55	6.05	13	35.38	5.3	53	36.69	5.45	0.90	0.79
Rayagada	23	34.78	7.49	33	39.77	9.93	47	31.01	8.67	1.87	4.09 **

$^{*}p<.05$, $^{**}p<.01$

in Mathematics achievement and in Dhenkanal the reverse was true. In the remaining two districts (Kalahandi and Gajapati), there was hardly any difference between ST and others.

SECTION E : COMPARATIVE PROFILES OF STUDENTS' ACHIEVEMENT ON BAS DURING INITIAL AND MID-TERM SURVEY (MAS)

One of the objectives of the study was to compare the average performance of students achievement on the BAS Tests administered during the initial survey in 1996 with that of students' performance on the same Tests re-administered during MAS in 1999 of the five DPEP districts, namely Bolangir, Dhenkanal, Gajapati, Kalahandi and Rayagada. Such comparison would reveal gain or loss or even statuesque in respect of students' achievement in language and Mathematics. Besides, this comparison would throw some light on the impact of DPEP interventions. Hence, the investigator thought of to re-analyse the data collected under the MAS by Directorate, TE and SCERT, ORISSA. The MAS was conducted by Directorate, TE and SCERT, Orissa in 1999 to make a comparative assessment of the students' achievement (Language and Mathematics) in the BAS (1996) Tests and that of students achievement (Language and Mathematics), in the same tests during MAS (1999).

The sample for these studies comprised students of class I and class IV of the five project districts. Hence, an attempt is made here by the investigator to re-analyse the achievement of classes I and IV students in Language and Mathematics under the BAS and MAS Tests.

Comparative position of class I students in Language is given in Table 5.26.

Students' performance (vide Table 5.26) showed significantly positive difference in three out of five districts with one district (Rayagada) showing loss of achievement by nearly two per cent. The hike in achievement went upto as much as twenty percentage points in Bolangir district. In Gajapati district there was no significant difference in language achievement. Three districts (Bolangir, Dhenkenal and Kalahandi) showed

Table 5.26 Genderwise Comparison of Achievement of Class I Students in Language on the BAS Test Administered During the Initial Survey and Mid-Term Survey

District	Gender	Initial Survey				Mid -Term Survey				Significance (CR value)	
		N	Mean %	SD	SE_M	N	Mean %	SD	SE_M		
Balangir	Boys	230	54.35	3.75	0.25	65	69.08	6.44	0.80	17.62	**
	Girls	201	45.80	3.71	0.26	65	71.54	5.72	0.71	34.04	**
	Total	431	50.35	3.72	0.18	130	70.31	6.09	0.53	35.43	**
Dhenkanal	Boys	298	69.60	4.19	0.20	70	77.07	5.59	0.67	10.70	**
	Girls	225	67.20	3.68	0.25	8.1	80.25	4.48	0.50	23.51	**
	Total	523	68.85	3.53	0.15	151	78.77	5.03	0.41	22.67	**
Gajapati	Boys	215	71.50	3.31	0.23	76	71.84	6.08	0.70	0.46	
	Girls	117	74.25	3.48	0.32	35	72.71	6.36	1.07	1.37	
	Total	332	72.50	3.33	0.18	111	72.12	6.17	0.59	0.62	
Kalahandi	Boys	239	44.20	4.19	0.27	52	60.29	7.15	0.99	15.65	**
	Girls	159	45.10	4.15	0.33	52	62.02	6.77	0.94	17.01	**
	Total	398	44,55	4.16	0.21	104	61.15	6.96	0.68	23.26	**
Rayagada	Boys	277	65.60	3.74	0.22	71	63.45	5.71	0.68	3.01	**
	Girls	164	62.55	4.15	0.32	59	61.53	6.91	0.90	1.07	
	Total	441	64,45	3.75	0.18	130	62.58	6.28	0.55	3.23	**

* $P<.05$, **$P<.01$.

significant positive improvement in achievement in Language, the gain being as much as twenty per cent. So the hypothesis (2.4.7) is partly accepted and partly rejected.

Comparative profiles of mathematics achievement difference between BAS and MAS for boys and girls have been presented in Table 5.27.

It is evident from Table 5.27 that students of Class-I in all districts had demonstrated significantly positive trends in achievement in Mathematics. The maximum gain was 13 points with minimum gain of two points. This shows the efficacy of DPEP interventions very clearly. So the hypothesis (*i.e.,* 2.4.8 in case of class I) is accepted.

Comparative position of class IV students in Language is given in Table 5.28.

The results as projected in Table 5.28 conclude that the students in four districts had significant gains in the MAS over the BAS. The magnitude of this gain was as much as 18 percentage points in Dhenkanal, which is quite high. Only in one district (*i.e.,* Rayagada) there was statusquo in language achievement. Hence, the hypothesis (*i.e.,* 2.4.7) is partly accepted and partly rejected.

Comparative profile of achievement in mathematics for boys and girls of Class IV are given in Table 5.29

Mean percentage of achievement in mathematics (vide Table 5.29) showed mixed findings. In three out of five districts (Bolangir, Kalahandi and Rayagada) there were significant losses in achievement scores (Mathematics) to the extent of three to nine per cent. In the remaining two districts, there was significant gains which varied from seven per cent to twelve per cent. So the hypothesis (*i.e.,* 2.4.8) in case of class IV is accepted.

SECTION F : COMPARISON OF LEARNERS' ACHIEVEMENT ON THE NEWLY GENERATED COMPETENCY-BASED ACHIEVEMENT TESTS IN ORIYA LANGUAGE/MATHEMATICS AND EVS OF THE DPEP AND NON-DPEP DISTRICTS

The final objective of the study was to compare the performance of learners' achievement on the newly generated

Table 5.27 : Gender-wise Comparison of Achievement of Class I Students in Mathematics on the BAS Test Administered During the Initial Survey and Mid-Term Survey

District	Gender	Initial Survey				Mid -Term Survey				Significance (CR value)
		N	Mean %	SD	Sem	N	Mean %	SD	Sem	
Balangir	Boys	230	53.29	2.33	0.15	65	62.74	3.98	0.49	18.28**
	Girls	20-1	44.71	2.31	0.16	65	61.42	3.6	0.45	35.16**
	Total	431	49.36	3.96	0.19	130	62.08	3.79	0.33	33.19**
Dhenkanal	Boys	298	69.57	2.35	0.14	70	79.79	3.82	0.46	21.45**
	Girls	225	64.71	2.46	0.16	81	72.48	4.00	0.44	16.40**
	Total	523	67.50	2.40	0.10	151	75.87	3.92	0.32	24.92**
Gajapati	Boys	215	67.43	2.51	0.17	76	65.03	4.12	0.47	4.77**
	Girls	117	63.00	2.76	0.26	35	71.42	4.36	0.74	10.80**
	Total	332	65.93	2.62	0.14	111	67.05	4.20	0.40	2.64**
Kalahandi	Boys	239	42.64	2.81	0.18	52	52.82	4.51	0.63	17.20**
	Girls	159	41.71	3.83	0.30	52	48.76	4.46	0.62	10.23**
	Total	398	42.63	3.92	0.20	104	51.30	4.49	0.44	18.54**
Rayagada	Boys	277	60.00	2.65	0.16	71	69.11	3.60	0.43	19.98**
	Girls	164	56.43	2.80	0.22	59	69.24	4.17	0.54	21.86**
	Total	441	58.64	2.70	0.13	130	69.17	3.87	0.34	29.01**

*P<.05, **P<01.

Table 5.28 : Gender-wise Comparison of Achievement of Class IV Students in Language on the BAS Test Administered During the Initial Survey and Mid-Term Survey

District	Gender	Initial Survey				Mid-Term Survey				Significance (CR value)
		N	Mean %	SD	Sem	N	Mean %	SD	Sem	
Balangir	Boys	255	34.60	5.79	0.36	51	42.88	14.93	2.09	3.90**
	Girls	107	35.13	6.61	0.64	50	40.23	13.18	1.86	2.58*
	Total	362	34.75	6.04	0.32	101	41.57	14.09	1.40	4.74**
Dhenkanal	Boys	285	41.53	6.94	0.41	80	59.64	15.30	1.71	10.29**
	Girls	244	37.55	5.51	0.35	75	55.46	16.51	1.91	9.23**
	Total	529	39.73	6.37	0.28	155	57.61	15.90	1.28	13.68**
Gajapati	Boys	164	41.23	6.03	0.47	56	53.72	18.00	2.41	5.09**
	Girls	72	45.40	7.22	0.85	29	54.55	17.53	3.26	2.71**
	Total	236	42.50	6.45	0.42	85	54.00	17.84	1.94	5.80**
Kalahandi	Boys	185	30.03	4.95	0.36	43	44.26	12.57	1.92	7.29**
	Girls	97	32.15	4.95	0.50	59	41.00	10.56	1.37	6.04**
	Total	282	30.75	4.97	0.30	102	42.37	11.45	1.13	9.91**
Rayagada	Boys	267	39.70	6.46	0.40	47	38.27	21.15	3.08	0.45
	Girls	125	42.00	5.73	0.51	56	42.09	16.93	2.26	0.03
	Total	392	40.45	6.25	0.32	103	40.34	18.97	1.87	0.05

*P<.05, **P<.01

Table 5.29 : Gender-wise Comparison of Achievement of Class IV Students in mathematics on the BAS Test Administered during the Initial Survey and Mid-Term Survey

District	Gen-der	Initial Survey				Mid -Term Survey				Significance (CR value)
		N	Mean %	SD	Sem	N	Mean %	SD	Sem	
Balangir	Boys	255	41.72	7.68	0.48	51	39.01	8.50	1.19	2.14**
	Girls	107	40.18	7.90	0.76	50	37.15	9.35	1.32	1.98*
	Total	362	41.27	7.68	0.40	101	38.09	8.93	0.89	3.25**
Dhenkanal	Boys	285	43.56	7.12	0.42	80	57.12	9.50	1.06	11.86**
	Girls	244	41.17	6.63	0.42	75	51.76	8.43	0.97	2.79**
	Total	529	42.94	6.20	0.27	155	54.53	9.00	0.72	15.02**
Gajapati	Boys	164	38.01	7.10	0.55	56	46.16	7.55	1.01	7.07**
	Girls	72	41.75	7.49	0.88	29	49.13	10.32	1.92	3.49**
	Total	236	39.74	7.86	0.51	85	47.17	8.59	0.93	6.99**
Kalahandi	Boys	185	39.50	6.41	0.47	43	36.86	5.47	0.83	2.75**
	Girls	97	43.13	6.12	0.70	59	35.59	5.21	0.68	7.72**
	Total	282	41.37	7.30	0.43	102	36.12	5.32	0.53	7.68**
Rayagada	Boys	267	43.43	6.35	0.39	47	31.96	10.09	1.47	7.53**
	Girls	125	46.93	6.22	0.46	56	36.91	7.42	99	8.81**
	Total	392	43.90	6.45	0.33	103	34.66	8.74	0.86	10.03**

*P<.05, **P<.0|

competency-based achievement tests in oriya language, mathematics and EVS at the end of Class III and Class V in the four DPEP districts (*i.e.*, Bolangir, Gajapati, Dhenkanal and Kalahandi) and three Non-DPEP districts (*i.e.*, Ganjam, Puri and Balasore) of Orissa. In this context, relevant hypotheses (*i.e.*, 2.4.9 and 2.4.10) have been formulated. For the purpose competency-based achievement tests in Oriya language, mathematics and EVS for the learners of Class III and Class V have been separately constructed. These tests were administered over the selected sample to obtain relevant data. The distribution of scores on the newly generated competency-based achievement tests in Oriya language, mathematics and EVS for the sample students were examined in respect of their nature and departure from normalcy. In this context, Skewness and Kurtosis were computed following the percentile method (Garrett, 1981). Table 5.30 shows the findings in this regard.

Table 5.30 : Values of Skewness and Kurtosis of Newly Generated Competency-based Tests

Subjects	DPEP Districts		Non-DPEP Districts	
	SK	KU	SK	KU
Oriya Language	0.07	0.15	0.04	0.20
Mathematics	0.03	0.21	0.06	0.13
EVS	0.09	0.17	1.14	0.19

The values of Skewness and Kurtosis in Table 5.30 indicated normality.

In pursuance of the objective of the study (*i.e.*, 2.3.8), the obtained data were subjected to statistical analysis considered appropriate (*i.e.*, t-test) to test the hypotheses (*i.e.*, 2.4.9 and 2.4.10). In the following section results are summarized seriatim and discussed for each Class (*i.e.*, Class III and V) separately.

Mean scores, S.D. and 't' values (*i.e.*, in Oriya language) for class III students for the various group combinations generated by gender (boys and girls), area (rural and urban) and caste (SC and S.T. and General) of the DPEP and Non-DPEP districts are given in Table 5.31.

Table 5.31 : Comparison of Achievement of Class III Students in Language of DPEP and Non-DPEP Districts

Group	DPEP			NON DPEP				
	No. of students 'N'	Mean	SD	Group	No. of students 'N'	Mean	SD	't' values
Boys (Rural)	103	14.21	5.44	Boys (Rural)	92	14.93	7.46	0.76
Girls (Rural)	96	10.09	6.14	Girls (Rural)	82	14.98	6.37	5.82**
SC/ST (Rural)	96	10.56	5.56	SC/ST (Rural)	52	14.92	7.30	3.63**
B&G (Rural)	199	12.01	5.94	B&G (Rural)	174	14.85	6.96	4.52**
Boys (Urban)	104	14.58	5.99	Boys (Urban)	123	11.73	5.52	3.70**
Girls (Urban)	108	13.13	6.99	Girls (Urban)	124	11.42	6.75	1.88
SC/ST (Urban)	63	12.85	6.37	SC/ST (Urban)	42	11.46	6.61	1.04
B&G (Urban)	212	13.80	6.56	B&G (Urban)	247	12.07	6.16	2.21*
Boys (Rural + Urban)	207	14.21	5.44	Boys (Rural + Urban)	215	13.33	6.61	1.49
Girls (Rural + Urban)	204	11.61	6.14	Girls (Rural + Urban)	206	13.2	6.83	2.47*
SC/ST (Rural + Urban)	159	11.44	5.56	SC/ST (Rural + Urban)	94	12.96	7.15	1.76
Boys (Rural + Urban)	207	14.21	5.44	Girls (Rural + Urban)	206	13.2	6.83	1.66
Girls (Rural + Urban)	204	11.61	6.14	Boys (Rural + Urban)	215	13.33	6.61	2.78**
Boys (Rural)	103	14.21	5.44	Boys (Urban)	123	11.73	5.52	3.39**

Group	DPEP No. of students 'N'	DPEP Mean	DPEP SD	NON DPEP Group	NON DPEP No. of students 'N'	NON DPEP Mean	NON DPEP SD	't' values
Girls (Rural)	96	10.09	6.14	Girls (Urban)	124	11.42	6.75	1.52
SC/ST (Rural)	96	10.56	5.56	SC/ST (Urban)	42	11.46	6.61	0.77
B+G (Rural)	199	12.01	5.94	B+G (Urban)	247	11.07	6.16	0.10
Boys (Urban)	104	14.58	5.99	Boys (Rural)	92	14.93	7.46	0.36
Girls (Urban)	108	13.13	6.99	Girls (Rural)	82	14.98	6.37	1.91
SC/ST (Urban)	63	12.85	6.37	SC/ST (Rural)	52	14.92	7.30	1.60
B+G (Urban)	212	13.80	6.56	B+G (Rural)	174	14.85	6.96	1.51
General (B+G)	252	13.68	4.83	General (B+G)	327	13.66	5.67	0.05
Total	411	12.94	5.94	Total	421	13.26	6.71	0.72

*p < .05 and **p < .01.

The mean score in Oriya language of rural girls belonging to Non-DPEP districts were found as 14.98 which is the highest mean score in comparison to other groups. On the other hand, rural girls of DPEP districts are found at the lower level (M = 10.09). Statistical analysis reveals that there is no significant difference in the learners' performance (*i.e.,* language) of DPEP and Non-DPEP districts. Hence, the hypothesis *i.e.,* 2.4.9 (i) was rejected. It indicates that the learners of class III belonging to DPEP and Non-DPEP districts occupied the similar position in the language achievement. However, significant differences in the mean scores of achievement of class III Children of DPEP and Non-DPEP districts in Oriya language were noted for the different sub-groups/namely girls from rural area (t = 5.82, P < .01), SC/ST belonging to rural area (t = 3.63, P < 01), both boys and girls of rural area (t = 4.52, P < .01), boys from urban area (t = 3.70, P < .01), both boys and girls from urban areas (t = 2.21, P < .05), girls from both rural and urban areas (t = 2.54, P <. 05), girls from rural and urban, and boys from rural and urban (t = 2.78, P < .01), and boys of rural and urban areas (t = 3.08, P < .01). On the basis of the comparison of their mean scores it can be concluded that the rural girls, the rural SC/ST students, the rural boys and girls, the boys and girls from both the rural and urban areas of Non-DPEP districts appeared to be superior in the achievement in oriya language than their respective DPEP counterparts. However, language achievement of urban and rural boys and even both boys and girls from urban areas of DPEP districts was significantly greater than their respective Non-DPEP counterparts. This reflects the efficacy of DPEP interventions very clearly. Hence, the hypothesis (*i.e.,* 2.4.9 (i)) is rejected.

Table 5.32 : Comparison of Achievement of Class III Students in Mathematics of DPEP and Non-DPEP Districts

	DPEP			NON DPEP				
Group	No. of students 'N'	Mean	SD	Group	No. of students 'N'	Mean	SD	't' values
Boys (Rural)	103	13.87	4.59	Boys (Rural)	92	15.66	5.67	2.40*
Girls (Rural)	96	12.03	5.23	Girls (Rural)	82	14.89	5.88	3.40**
SC/ST (Rural)	96	12.05	4.81	SC/ST (Rural)	52	15.40	5.95	3.48**
B&G (Rural)	199	13.13	4.98	B&G (Rural)	174	15.27	5.78	3.80**
Boys (Urban)	104	12.96	5.31	Boys (Urban)	123	13.61	4.78	0.96
Girls (Urban)	108	11.78	4.5	Girls (Urban)	124	13.27	5.92	1.99
SC/ST (Urban)	63	11.49	5.80	SC/ST (Urban)	42	11.87	6.13	0.32
B&G (Urban)	212	12.69	5.52	B&G (Urban)	247	13.44	5.38	1.47

Group	DPEP No. of students 'N'	DPEP Mean	DPEP SD	Group	NON DPEP No. of students 'N'	NON DPEP Mean	NON DPEP SD	't' values
Boys (Rural + Urban)	207	14.46	4.36	Boys Rural + Urban)	215	14.63	5.28	0.36
Girls (Rural + Urban)	204	11.92	5.12	Girls (Rural +Urban)	206	14.08	5.96	3.94**
SC/ST (Rural +Urban)	159	11.78	5.47	SC/ST (Rural +Urban)	94	13.63	6.28	2.37*
Boys (Rural +Urban)	207	14.46	4.36	Girls (Rural +Urban)	206	14.08	5.96	0.74
Girls (Rural +Urban)	204	11.92	5.12	Boys (Rural +Urban)	215	14.63	5.28	5.33**
Boys (Rural)	103	13.87	4.59	Boys (Urban)	123	13.61	4.78	0.42
Girls (Rural)	96	12.03	5.23	Girls (Urban)	124	13.27	5.92	1.65
SC/ST (Rural)	96	12.05	4.81	SC/ST (Urban)	42	11.87	6.13	0.17
B+G (Rural)	199	13.13	4.98	B+G (Urban)	247	13.44	5.38	0.63
Boys (Urban)	104	12.96	5.31	Boys (Rural)	92	15.66	5.67	3.43**
Girls (Urban)	108	11.78	5.45	Girls (Rural)	82	14.89	5.88	3.73**
SC/ST (Urban)	63	11.49	5.80	SC/ST (Rural)	52	15.40	5.95	3.55**
B+G (Urban)	212	12.69	5.52	B+G (Rural)	174	15.27	5.78	4.45**
General (B+G)	252	13.53	4.93	General (B+G)	327	16.25	4.61	3.97**
Total	411	12.85	5.29	Total	421	14.35	5.62	3.96**

*p < .05 and **p <.01.

Comparative profile of achievement scores in mathematics for the learners of class III of DPEP and Non-DPEP districts are given in Table 5.32. An examination of the data presented in Table 5.32 indicates that the learners of class III of DPEP and Non-DPEP districts vary significantly in their mathematics achievement and difference goes in favour of the learners of Non-DPEP districts. Hence, it can be concluded that the learners of class III of Non-DPEP districts achieved significantly greater gain in mathematics achievement than their DPEP counterparts. In view of the above result, the hypothesis *i.e.*, 2.4.9 (ii) was retained. Similar was the situation with certain sub-groups. The inter group comparisons suggest that the learners of class III of Non-DPEP districts achieved significantly higher in the mathematics achievement than their DPEP counterparts. This poses challenges to the efficacy of DPEP interventions. Hence, the hypothesis *i.e.*, 2.4.9. (ii) is accepted.

Table 5.33 : Comparison of Achievement of Class III Students in EVS of DPEP and Non-DPEP Districts

	DPEP			NON DPEP				
Group	**No. of students 'N'**	**Mean**	**SD**	**Group**	**No. of students 'N'**	**Mean**	**SD**	**'t' values**
Boys (Rural)	103	13.01	5.74	Boys (Rural)	92	15.06	6.14	2.41*
Girls (Rural)	96	10.85	6.35	Girls (Rural)	82	14.41	5.55	4.14**
SC/ST (Rural)	96	10.58	6.15	SC/ST (Rural)	52	14.69	5.69	4.10**
B&G (Rural)	199	12.1	6.16	B&G (Rural)	174	14.73	5.88	4.20**
Boys (Urban)	104	13.52	6.84	Boys (Urban)	123	12.31	5.05	1.49
Girls (Urban)	108	11.93	6.93	Girls (Urban)	124	12.07	5.29	0.17
SC/ST (Urban)	63	11.71	7.61	SC/ST (Urban)	42	11.64	5.44	0.06
B&G (Urban)	212	12.73	6.93	B&G (Urban)	247	12.19	5.17	0.93

Group	DPEP No. of students 'N'	DPEP Mean	DPEP SD	Group	NON DPEP No. of students 'N'	NON DPEP Mean	NON DPEP SD	't' values
Boys (Rural +Urban)	207	13.27	6.32	Boys (Rural +Urban)	215	13.68	5.71	0.71
Girls (Rural +Urban)	204	11.40	6.67	Girls (Rural +Urban)	206	13.24	5.51	3.07**
SC/ST (Rural +Urban)	159	11.15	6.79	SC/ST (Rural +Urban)	94	13.16	5.78	2.54*
Boys (Rural +Urban)	207	13.27	6.32	Girls (Rural +Urban)	206	13.24	5.51	0.05
Girls (Rural +Urban)	204	11.40	6.67	Boys (Rural +Urban)	215	13.68	5.71	3.81**
Boys (Rural)	103	13.01	5.74	Boys (Urban)	123	12.31	5.05	1.57
Girls (Rural)	96	10.85	6.35	Girls (Urban)	124	12.07	5.29	1.56
SC/ST (Rural)	96	10.58	6.15	SC/ST (Urban)	42	11.64	5.44	1.03
B+G (Rural)	199	12.1	6.16	B+G (Urban)	247	12.19	5.17	0.17
Boys (Urban)	104	13.52	6.84	Boys (Rural)	92	15.06	6.14	1.66
Girls (Urban)	108	11.93	6.93	Girls (rural)	82	14.41	5.55	2.75**
SC/ST (Urban)	63	11.71	7.61	SC/ST (Rural)	52	14.69	5.69	2.70**
B+G (Urban)	212	12.73	6.93	B+G (Rural)	174	14.73	5.88	3.07**
General (B+G)	252	12.27	5.87	General (B+G)	327	13.25	5.11	2.09*
Total	411	12.42	6.58	Total	421	13.46	5.62	2.36*

*p < .05, **p <.01.

A perusal of Table 5.33 shows that the learners of Class III of DPEP and Non-DPEP districts differed significantly with respect to their achievement in environmental science ($t = 2.36$, $p < .05$). Hence the hypothesis *i.e.,* 2.4.9 (iii) was accepted. These differences were in favour of the learners of Class III of Non-DPEP districts. Thus, it can be said that the students of Class 111 belonging to Non-DPEP districts had demonstrated significantly positive trends in EVS achievement. In case of DPEP districts, there is a loss of achievement in EVS by 1.04 per cent, which is significant. When the achievement in EVS of the learners of Class III, grouped in terms of gender, area and caste, was compared, it was found that the learners of DPEP districts achieved significantly lower than that of their Non-DPEP counter parts. So the hypothesis *i.e.,* 2.4.9 (iii) is retained.

Table 5.34 : Comparison of Class V Students in Language of DPEP and Non-DPEP Districts

	DPEP			NON DPEP				
Group	No. of students 'N'	Mean	SD	Group	No. of students 'N'	Mean	SD	't' values
Boys (Rural)	83	13.39	5.19	Boys (Rural)	66	13.18	6.19	0.02
Girls (Rural)	135	11.10	5.72	Girls (Rural)	79	9.99	5.66	1.70
SC/ST (Rural)	84	11.57	5.39	SC/ST (Rural)	41	9.88	6.09	1.52
B&G (Rural)	218	11.91	5.46	B&G (Rural)	145	11.76	6.08	0.15
Boys (Urban)	86	11.53	4.13	Boys (Urban)	150	11.58	5.43	0.08
Girls (Urban)	121	10.53	4.64	Girls (Urban)	143	12.34	4.96	3.04**
SC/ST (Urban)	61	9.68	3.51	SC/ST (Urban)	46	11.78	4.43	2.66**
B&G (Urban)	208	11.02	4.46	B&G (Urban)	293	11.96	4.63	5.52**

Group	DPEP No. of students 'N'	DPEP Mean	DPEP SD	Group	NON DPEP No. of students 'N'	NON DPEP Mean	NON DPEP SD	't' values
Boys (Rural +Urban)	169	12.43	4.89	Boys (Rural +Urban)	216	12.38	5.85	0.09
Girls (Rural +Urban)	257	10.73	5.10	Girls (Rural +Urban)	222	11.17	5.35	0.92
SC/ST (Rural +Urban)	145	10.74	4.91	SC/ST (Rural +Urban)	87	10.83	5.12	0.13
Boys (Rural +Urban)	169	12.43	4.89	Girls (Rural +Urban)	222	11.17	5.35	2.42*
Girls (Rural +Urban)	257	10.73	5.10	Boys (Rural +Urban)	216	12.38	5.85	3.23**
Boys (Rural)	83	13.39	5.19	Boys (Urban)	150	11.58	5.43	2.51*
Girls (Rural)	135	11.10	5.72	Girls (Urban)	143	12.34	4.96	1.92
SC/ST (Rural)	84	11.57	5.39	SC/ST (Urban)	46	11.78	4.43	0.39
B+G (Rural)	218	11.91	5.46	B+G (Urban)	293	11.96	4.63	0.11
Boys (Urban)	86	11.53	4.13	Boys (Rural)	66	13.18	6.19	1.86
Girls (Urban)	122	10.53	4.64	Girls (Rural)	79	9.99	5.66	0.70
SC/ST (Urban)	61	9.68	3.51	SC/ST (Rural)	41	9.88	6.09	0.19
B+G (Urban)	208	11.02	4.46	B+G (Rural)	145	11.76	6.08	1.24
General (B+G)	281	11.80	5.08	General (B+G)	351	12.00	5.23	0.48
Total	426	11.54	5.09	Total	438	11.86	5.29	0.90

*p < .05 and **p <.01.

A perusal of Table 5.34 shows that the learners' of Class V of DPEP and Non-DPEP district did not differ significantly with respect to their achievement in Oriya language (t = 0.90). Hence, the hypothesis *i.e.,* 2.4.10 (i) was rejected. Thus it can be said that the students of Class V belonging to both DPEP and Non-DPEP districts occupied the similar position in Oriya language achievement. However, in case of DPEP districts, there is a loss of achievement in Oriya Language by 0.32 per cent, which is not significant. When the achievement in Oriya language of the learners of Class V, grouped in terms of gender, caste and area, was compared, it was found that the learners' of DPEP districts achieved significantly lower than that of the learners of their Non-DPEP counterparts (excepting boys of DPEP vs. girls of Non-DPEP, and rural boys of DPEP vs. urban boys of Non-DPEP districts). The boys of DPEP districts achieved significantly higher than the girls of Non-DPEP districts and the boys of Rural DPEP districts also achieved significantly higher than that of the boys of Urban Non-DPEP districts.

So the hypothesis 2.4.10 (i) is rejected.

Table 5.35 : Comparison of Class V Students in Mathematics of DPEP and Non-DPEP Districts

	DPEP			NON DPEP				
Group	No. of students 'N'	Mean	SD	Group	No. of students 'N'	Mean	SD	't' values
Boys (Rural)	83	12.55	5.20	Boys (Rural)	66	13.30	6.97	0.71
Girls (Rural)	135	9.46	5.06	Girls (Rural)	79	10.32	6.06	1.06
SC/ST (Rural)	84	11.45	5.94	SC/ST (Rural)	41	9.97	5.66	1.35
B&G (Rural)	218	10.67	5.36	B&G (Rural)	145	11.62	6.64	1.44
Boys (Urban)	86	12.75	3.69	Boys (Urban)	150	13.03	5.15	0.79
Girls (Urban)	122	10.57	3.63	Girls (Urban)	143	12.87	4.99	4.33**

DPEP				NON DPEP				
Group	No. of students 'N'	Mean	SD	Group	No. of students 'N'	Mean	SD	't' values
SC/ST (Urban)	61	11.13	3.67	SC/ST (Urban)	46	13.02	5.94	1.91
B&G (Urban)	208	11.5	3.75	B&G (Urban)	293	12.95	5.05	1.66
Boys (Rural +Urban)	169	12.70	4.44	Boys (Rural +Urban)	216	13.04	5.82	0.71
Girls (Rural +Urban)	257	9.98	5.61	Girls (Rural +Urban)	222	12.41	8.58	1.06
SC/ST (Rural +Urban)	145	11.32	1.38	SC/ST (Rural +Urban)	87	10.26	5.95	1.35
Boys (Rural +Urban)	169	12.70	4.44	Girls (Rural +Urban)	222	12.41	8.58	0.43
Girls (Rural +Urban)	257	9.98	5.61	Boys (Rural +Urban)	216	13.04	5.82	5.79**
Boys (Rural)	83	12.55	5.20	Boys (Urban)	150	13.03	5.15	0.67
Girls (Rural)	135	9.46	5.06	Girls (Urban)	143	12.87	4.99	5.65**
SC/ST (Rural)	84	11.45	5.94	SC/ST (Urban)	46	13.02	5.94	1.44
B+G (Rural)	218	10.67	5.36	B+G (Urban)	293	12.95	5.05	4.87**
Boys (Urban)	86	12.75	3.69	Boys (Rural)	66	13.30	6.97	0.77
Girls (Urban)	122	10.57	3.63	Girls (Rural)	79	10.32	6.06	0.33
SC/ST (Urban)	61	11.13	3.67	SC/ST (Rural)	41	9.97	5.66	1.16
B+G (Urban)	208	11.5	3.75	B+G (Rural)	145	11.62	6.64	0.19
General (B+G)	281	10.88	4.38	General (B+G)	351	12.74	5.81	4.59**
Total	426	11.07	4.67	Total	438	13.77	5.68	1.44

*p < .05 and **p <. 01.

Comparative profile of achievement scores in mathematics for learners of Class V of DPEP and Non-DPEP districts are given in Table 5.35. An examination of the data presented in Table 5.35 indicates that the learners of Class V of DPEP and Non-DPEP districts did not differ significantly in their achievement in mathematics (t =1.35). Hence, it can be concluded that there is no significant difference in the mathematics achievement of learners of Class V of DPEP and Non-DPEP districts on newly generated competency-based test. In view of the above result, the hypothesis *i.e.,* 2.4.10 (ii) was rejected. Similar was situation with certain sub groups. The inter group comparison indicate that the learners of Class V of Non-DPEP districts achieved significantly higher in the mathematics achievement than their counterparts. Thus it would tend to mean that DPEP interventions have failed in its mission with respected to certain groups in terms of gender and area. This poses a challenge to the efficacy of DPEP interventions. So the hypothesis 2.4.10 (ii) is rejected.

Table 5.36 : Comparison of Achievement of Class V Students in EVS of DPEP and Non-DPEP Districts.

Group	DPEP No. of students "N"	DPEP Mean	DPEP SD	Group	NON DPEP No. of students 'N'	NON DPEP Mean	NON DPEP SD	't' values
Boys (Rural)	83	13.80	5.86	Boys (Rural)	66	11.78	6.23	4.13**
Girls (Rural)	135	11.06	5.7	Girls (Rural)	79	8.42	8.42	5.70**
SC/ST (Rural)	84	12.06	5.97	SC/ST (Rural)	41	8.76	5.99	5.97**
B&G (Rural)	218	12.28	5.84	B&G (Rural)	145	9.43	6.02	5.84**
Boys (Urban)	86	11.91	4.32	Boys (Urban)	150	11.26	4.03	1.14
Girls (Urban)	122	10.08	6.50	Girls (Urban)	143	10.94	4.54	1.23
SC/ST (Urban)	61	9.64	4.27	SC/ST (Urban)	46	10.93	5.32	1.36

Group	DPEP No. of students 'N'	DPEP Mean	DPEP SD	NON DPEP Group	NON DPEP No. of students 'N'	NON DPEP Mean	NON DPEP SD	't' values
B&G (Urban)	208	10.57	4.32	B&G (Urban)	293	11.19	4.25	1.59
Boys (Rural +Urban)	169	12.91	5.17	Boys (Rural +Urban)	182	11.52	5.24	4.13**
Girls (Rural +Urban)	257	10.42	5.03	Girls (Rural +Urban)	222	9.68	10.28	2.28*
SC/ST (Rural +Urban)	145	12.19	6.15	SC/ST (Rural +Urban)	87	9.92	5.78	2.92**
Boys (Rural +Urban)	169	12.91	5.17	Girls (Rural +Urban)	222	9.68	10.28	3.94**
Girls (Rural +Urban)	257	10.42	5.03	Boys (Rural +Urban)	216	11.52	5.24	0.35
Boys (Rural)	83	13.80	5.86	Boys (Urban)	150	11.26	4.03	3.49**
Girls (Rural)	135	11.06	5.7	Girls (Urban)	143	10.94	4.54	0.19
SC/ST (Rural)	84	12.06	5.97	SC/ST (Urban)	46	10.93	5.32	1.11
B+G (Rural)	218	12.28	5.84	B+G (Urban)	293	11.19	4.25	2.33*
Boys (Urban)	86	11.91	4.32	Boys (Rural)	66	11.78	6.23	0.11
Girls (Urban)	122	10.08	6.50	Girls (Rural)	79	8.42	8.42	1.37
SC/ST (Urban)	61	9.64	4.27	SC/ST (Rural)	41	8.76	5.99	0.82
B+G (Urban)	208	10.57	4.3'2	B+G (Rural)	145	9.43	6.02	1.67
General (B+G)	281	11.64	5.11	General (B+G)	351	10.79	7.23	1.81
Total	426	11.38	5.33	Total	438	10.6	7.84	3.89**

*p < .05 and **p <.01.

Mean scores, S.D. and 't' values (*i.e.*, in EVS) for Class V students for the various group combinations generated by gender (boys and girls), area (Rural and Urban) and caste (SC, ST and general) of the DPEP and Non-DPEP districts are given in Table 5.36.

The mean score in EVS of rural boys belonging to Non-DPEP districts were found to be 11.78 which is the highest mean score in comparison to other groups. On the other hand, SC/ST students of urban areas of DPEP districts are found at the lower level (M = 9.64). Statistical analysis reveals that there is significant difference in the learners' performance (*i.e.*, EVS) of DPEP and Non-DPEP districts. Learners of Class V of DPEP and Non-DPEP districts vary significantly in their EVS achievement and the difference goes in favour of the learners of DPEP districts. Hence, it can be said that the learners of Class V of DPEP districts achieved significantly greater in EVS achievement than their Non-DPEP counterparts. In view of the above conclusion, the hypothesis *i.e.*, 2.4.10 (iii) was accepted. Significant differences on the mean scores of achievement of Class V children of DPEP and Non-DPEP districts in EVS were noted for different sub-groups, namely, boys from rural area (t = 4.13, P < .0.1), girls from rural area (t = 5.7. P < .01), SC/ST from rural area (t = 5.97, P <. 01), both boys and girls from rural area (t = 5.84, P <.01), boys of DPEP and Non DPEP districts (t = 4.13, P < .01), girls of DPEP and Non-DPEP districts (t = 2.28, P < .05), SC/ST of DPEP and Non-DPEP districts (t = 2.92, p < .01), and boys of DPEP district and girls of Non-DPEP districts (1 = 3.94, P < .01), rural boys of DPEP districts and urban boys of non-DPEP districts (1 = 3.49, P <. 01), and both boys and girls from rural areas of DPEP districts and boys and girls from rural areas of Non-DPEP districts (t = 2.33, P <. 05).

On the basis of the comparison of their mean scores it can be concluded that the rural boys, rural girls, rural SC/ST, rural boys and girls, SC/ST, boys and girls from both the rural and urban areas of DPEP districts appeared to be superior in the achievement in EVS than their respective Non-DPEP counterparts. This reflects the efficacy of DPEP interventions very clearly in the achievement in Environmental Science of the learners of Class V.

6

SUMMARY AND CONCLUSION

CONTEXT OF THE STUDY

Universalisation of Primary Education (UPE) in India, a constitutional mandate, has been persistently pursued, soon after becoming free from foreign dominion, in the form of numerous states and central programmes. The statesmen of India Keenly felt the exigency of universal primary education. Different measures taken by the Government to surmount the mammoth problem with the co-operation of all can help to solve the problem. Different agencies of the UNO have been extending helping hands to realise the goal of UPE. The historic document of NPE put a new thrust in primary education emphasizing universal enrolment and universal retention of children up to 14 years and qualitative improvement. NPE 1986 ensures that all children will be given free and compulsory Education up to 14 years. This gigantic effort requires co-operation of all to do away with the evil of illiteracy. Undoubtedly, this problem qualities for being ranked as the most fundamental problem of our educational system. Indian's primary education glass is two-third full, one-third empty (World Bank, 1997). The NPE (1986), Modified in 1992, made perhaps the first time, clear the enormity of the task of UPE by delineating its composite components as, (i) Universal access and enrolment, (ii) Universal retention of children until they attain the age of 14-years, and (iii) a substantial improvement in the learner achievement, the task of achieving UPE has become more daunting and challenging. Varghese (1995) remarked that the optimism on account of the expansion of the system diminishes progressively as one moves from enrolment to retention and again to levels of learner achievement at the primary stage. Recent studies on learner achievement at the primary level has shown Low levels of achievement (Dave *et al.*, 1988; Panda: 2000; Govinda and Varghese: 1993, Sukla: 1994; Mohanty: 1996).

With adoption of the NPE and POA, 1986 and 1992, quality and equity concerns began to occupy the centre-stage of primary education. Absence of decentralised planning till late 1980s and early 1990s has, in fact, exacerbated regional, gender and social group disparities. Despite of some efforts, since late eighty on wards, acceptance of district as a unit of planning has not emerged as a reality (except in DPEP districts) in the true sense of the term. The major constraints to initiate planning at the district level are: (i) Lack of resources base at the district level; (ii) Lack of planning competencies; and (iii) Absence of a planning machinery (Varghese: 1995).

The problem of reaching the hard core unreached stands a major stone wall to achieve the goals of UPE. Now, it is increasingly realised that, the traditional concept of expanding existing education systems-fails to recognize that these groups are precisely those who find such existing education systems unsuitable for their needs, their situations, their aspirations and their difficulties. Thus, educationally and socially disadvantaged and deprived children can not appropriately be met, by mainstream education. Hence, decentralised planning is what we are aiming as the only alternative to achieve the goal of UPE. The need that lies ahead in the march to UPE is a calling : (i) higher intensity of effort, and (ii) more systematic planning and implementation (GOI: 1995). Since the World Declaration on EFA (1990) at Jomitian Thailand, the international community and major UN agencies have developed a renewed interest in and commitment to accelerating the expansion of basic education for all. The World Bank and Department for International Development (DFID) supported District Primary Education Programme (DPEP) is an example of International commitment to the cause of UPE in India.

DPEP is, a home grown programme grounded on the country's own experience and built upon the experience acquired through the implementation of the Bihar Education Project,

UP Basic Education Project, AP Primary Education Project and Mahila Samakshya. In reality DPEP seeks to operationalise para 7.4.6 of the POA, 1992.

DPEP is the most ambitious programme so far, for the development of Primary Education in India. This programme launched in 1994 in 42 districts in 7 states, today it covers 15 states of more than 219 districts. DPEP builds upon accumulated national experience in the pursuit of UPE as well as experience gained from self specific and area specific project. DPEP is a home grown district specific programme emphasizing on access, retention and quality of learning.

DPEP was launched in Orissa in the second phase in 1996 with five districts namely Bolangir, Dhenkanal, Gajapati, Kalahandi and Rayagada. The programme was upscaled to another three districts: Baragarh, Keonjhar and Sambalpur in 1997. DPEP in these eight districts are being funded by the World Bank. The programme is being upscaled, to eight more districts: Koraoput, Malanigir, Nabarangpur, Boudh, Kandhamala, Mayurbhanj, Nuapada and Sonepur with DFID support. Six more district are in the way. Thus, within a year or two, twenty two out of thirty districts shall be joining the DPEP movement. The major initiatives undertaken in these districts under the auspices of DPEP in order to reform and renew the primary education system include the followings : (i) massive awareness generation programmes, generating social demand for schooling and genuine involvement and participation of community in school management; (ii) re-orienting the class room processes to make them interactive, child-centred, activity based and gender sensitive; (iii) improving the material and physical infrastructure of schools, making them conductive for their effective and efficient functioning; (iv) equipping school with teaching-learning materials to aid children's learning; (v) building educational and pedagogial capacity of teachers and educational supervisors for better performance, (vi) creatation of new structure such as VECs, MTAs, PTAs, and DIETs; (vii) strengthening and consolidating school community linkage; (viii) strengthening support system like NFE/alternative Schooling, IED and ECCE; (ix) Neutralising gender bias in curriculum, textbooks, school processes, and empowering women; and (x) taking up positive discriminatory measures in favour of socio-economically disadvantaged and deprived groups such as SCs and STs.

All these interventions and initiatives were directed towards reforming and renewing the primary education system in five first phase DPEP districts.

The DPEP intervention and strategies are based on the contextual realities and Local specific need and aspirations, identified through intense and involved consultative processes with the stakeholders.

DPEP interventions include: (a) Community mobilisation and participation, (b) Planning, Research and Evaluation, (c) Improved pedagogy, (d) School/village based programmes, (e) Institution building and building capacity, (f) Integrated education for the disabled, (g) Innovations, (h) Monitoring and supervision.

With all these interventions, it is felt that primary schools of DPEP districts would be turned into better performing schools.

OBJECTIVES OF THE STUDY

The following objectives were set forth for The investigation:

1. To find out if there were any impact of DPEP, Orissa on the access of the primary school children of five DPEP districts, namely, Bolangir, Gajapati, Kalahandi, Dhenkanal and Raygada taking the base line survey and data as parameters.
2. To find out if there were any impact of DPEP, Orissa on the retention of the primary school children of five DPEP districts, namely, Bolangir, Gajapati, Kalahandi, Dhenkanal and Raygada taking the Base line survey and data as parameters.
3. To assess the achievement of learners at the primary level of education in language and mathematics of those five DPEP districts as stated above on the BAS tests.
4. To study the differences among the learners of primary schools of those five DPEP districts (*i.e.*, Bolangir,

Gajapati, Kalahandi, Dhenkanal and Raygada.) due to gender, location and caste variations on the BAS tests.

5. To assess the performance of learners' achievement on the MAS in language and mathematics at the end of class 1 and at the end of penultimate class of primary schooling of those five DPEP districts.
6. To compare the achievement differences in regard to gender and social groups on MAS tests of those five DPEP districts.
7. To compare the average performance of learners' achievement on the BAS tests administered during the initial survey in 1996 with that of learners' performance on the same tests re-administered during MAS in 1999 of those five DPEP districts.
8. To compare the performance of learners' achievement on the newly generated competency - based achievement tests in language (*i.e.,* Oriya), mathematics and environmental studies at the end of class III and class V in the four DPEP districts (*i.e.,* Bolangir, Gajapati, Kalahandi arid Dhenkanal) and three Non-DPEP districts (*i.e.,* Ganjam, puri, and Balasore) of Orissa.

HYPOTHESES OF THE STUDY

Keeping in view the above objectives, the following hypotheses were formulated and tested under present study.

1. There is a positive impact of the District Primary Education Programme, Orissa on the access of the primary school children of five DPEP districts, namely, Bolangir, Gajapati, Kalahandi, Dhenkanal and Raygada.
2. There is a positive impact of the District Primary Education Programme, Orissa on the retention of the primary school children of five DPEP districts, namely, Bolangir, Gajapati, Kalahandi, Dhenkanal and Raygada.
3. There will be significant difference in the mean scores of achievement in Oriya language on the BAS Test

between: (i) boys and girls; (ii) rural and urban students; and (iii) SC/ST and Non-SC/ST students of those five DPEP districts of Orissa.

4. There will be significant difference in the mean scores of achievement in numeracy on the BAS test between: (i) Boys and girls; (ii) rural and urban students; and (iii) SC/ST and Non-SC/ST students of those five DPEP districts of Orissa.

5. There will be significant difference in the mean scores of achievement in Oriya language on the MAS test between: (i) boys and girls; (ii) urban and rural students; and (iii) SC/ST and Non-SC/ST students of those five DPEP districts of Orissa.

6. There will be significant difference in the mean scores of achievement in mathematics on the MAS test between: (i) boys and girls; (ii) rural and urban students; and (iii) SC/ST and Non-SC/ST students of those five DPEP districts of Orissa.

7. There will be significant difference in the mean scores of achievement in Oriya language on the BAS test and MAS test between boys and girls of class I and IV of those five DPEP districts of Orissa.

8. There will be significant difference in the mean scores of achievement in mathematics on the BAS test and MAS test between boys and girls of class I and IV of those five DPEP districts of Orissa.

9. There will be significant difference in the mean scores of achievement in class III children of DPEP and Non-DPEP districts on the newly generated competency-based test in (i) Oriya language, (ii) Mathematics, and (iii) EVS.

10. There will be significant difference in the mean scores of achievement in class V children of DPEP and Non-DPEP districts on the newly generated competency-based test in (i) Oriya language, (ii) Mathematics, and (iii) EVS.

COLLECTION OF DATA AND ITS TREATMENT

The subject of the study were the students of Primary schools of class III and class V-belonging to four DPEP districts (*i.e.*, Dhenkanal, Bolangir, Kalahandi and Gajapati) and three Non-DPEP districts (*i.e.*, Puri, Balasore and Ganjam) of Orissa. Relevant data were collected from 411 students of class III from DPEP districts; 421 students of class III from Non-DPEP districts; 426 students of class V from DPEP districts and 438 students of class V from Non-DPEP districts. The following tools were used for collecting relevant data.

(1) Achievement Test in Language, Mathematics and EVS for class III students.

(2) Achievement Test in Language, Mathematics and EVS for class V students.

Official documents like A base line Assessment study of Primary schools in Orissa, 1996 and a Mid-term Assessment Survey in Orissa, 1999 were collected and from Directorate, T.E. and S.C.E.R.T., Orissa.

The main purpose of the study was to study the impact of DPEP interventions on access, retention and achievement of students of primary grade belonging to project districts of Orissa. The data obtained were tabulated separately into frequency distribution. Mean and SD of each group were calculated. Comparison between different groups were made on the basis of the 't' test.

MAJOR FINDINGS

The preceding chapter has been devoted to the analysis and interpretation of data. The analyses have yielded some significant findings. Major findings have been presented under the following heads:

1. Findings pertaining to the impact of DPEP, Orissa on the access of the primary school children.
2. Findings pertaining to the impact of DPEP, Orissa on the retention of the primary school children.

3. Findings pertaining to the assessment and comparison of learners' achievement on BAS.
4. Findings pertaining to the assessment and comparison of Learners' achievement on MAS.
5. Findings pertaining to comparative profiles of students' achievement on BAS and MAS.
6. Findings pertaining to the study and comparison of the performance of learners' achievement on the newly generated competency-based achievement tests in language (Oriya), Mathematics and EVS at the end of Class III and Class V in the DPEP and Non-DPEP districts of Orissa.

Findings Pertaining to the Impact of DPEP, Orissa on the Access of the Primary School Children

1. There is an increase in the number of primary schools over the four years (1996-2000) from 5.83% to 22.39%. However, the rate of increase in the number of Primary schools in Dhenkanal district is found to be the highest and Rayagada the least out of the five project districts.
2. By the fruitful steps of DPEP the annual medical check up, immunization and First-Aid facilities in Primary Schools of the project districts have been increased over the four years.
3. The facilities like safe drinking water, separate toilet for boys and girls and electric connection have been improved in the project districts, namely, Gajapati (8%). Kalahandi (16%), Bolangir (20%), Dhenkanal and Rayagada (38%).
4. In the project districts most of the schools (*i.e.,* about 90%) have been provided with adequate infrastructures for effective teaching learning process.
5. During the period of 1996 to 2000 the percentage of female teachers has increased in all the project districts except in the district of Gajapati.

6. So far as SC teachers are concerned, an increasing trend has been visualised only in the project district like Bolangir. However, percentage of ST teachers is in increasing order only in one project district like Kalahandi. Similar is the situation of rural teacher. However, the number of urban teachers has been increased over the four years.
7. Percentage of trained (C.T.) female teachers has increased in all the project districts except Gajapati, whereas the trained (B.Ed.) female teachers has decreased in the districts like Bolangir, Kalahandi and Rayagada.
8. There is an overall decrease in the percentage of trained female teachers with M.Ed. degree in all the project districts where as there is a small increase only in the district of Kalahandi.

Findings Pertaining to the Impact of DPEP, Orissa on the retention of the Primary School Children

1. There is an increase in the percentage of enrolment of girls in all the project districts except Bolangir (Class III and V) and Rayagada (Class III).
2. Over the six-years (1996-2002) the enrolment of urban children is found to be increased, whereas for rural children it is decreased.
3. In all the project districts the percentage of enrolment of SC students has increased except in the district of Bolangir (for Class III) where as the percentage of enrolment of ST students has been increased in the two out of five project districts (*i.e.*, Dhenkanal and Gajapati).

Findings Pertaining to the Assessment and Comparison of Learners' Achievement on BAS

1. The average performance of the Class II students of Gajapati district in language was higher than their counterparts in the other four DPEP districts, namely, Bolangir, Dhenkanal, Kalahandi and Rayagada.

2. The performance of the Class II students of Bolangir and Kalahandi districts in language were located at the lowest end of the continuum.
3. The overall performance of students in numeracy across the DPEP districts, namely, Bolangir, Dhenkanal, Kalahandi, Rayagada and Gajapati was abnormally low. The performance of Class II students of Dhenkanal district in numeracy has highest average than their counterparts in the other four DPEP districts, namely, Bolangir, Kalahandi, Rayagada and Gajapati where as the performance of Class II students of Kalahandi district is minimum among the five DPEP districts.
4. The performance of students of Class II in Language was better as compared to numeracy.
5. The pattern of variation in the performance of students in Language across the DPEP districts was almost same as in numeracy.
6. The performance of students of Class II from Kalahandi and Bolangir was at the lowest ebb.
7. The gender difference in Letter Reading and Word Reading was not significant for any district except in Bolangir district.
8. The average performance in Language for students of Class II reading in urban schools were higher than their counterparts in rural schools.
9. Students of urban schools of Dhenkanal have highest average in both the components (*i.e.*, Letter Reading and word Reading) with minimum variance where as in rural schools of Kalahandi have lowest average with maximum variance.
10. The average performance of SC/ST students in Language was highest in Gajapati district and lowest in Kalahandi district.
11. In all the DPEP districts barring Bolangir, the inter-group difference between SC/ST and other groups in the

achievement of Language is significant *i.e.,* performance of the students belonging to SC and ST groups is lower than their counterparts in the general caste category.

12. The mean scores on numeracy of boys are more than that of girls.
13. In no district the gender difference is conspicuously significant in the achievement of numeracy except in Bolangir.
14. The average performance of students belonging to urban schools is higher in both the components of numeracy test (*i.e.,* Number Recognition and Addition and Subtraction) but there exists a significant difference in the performance of the students of rural and urban area schools in all DPEP districts except for Rayagada in the Number Recognition component.
15. The average performance of SC/ST students in numeracy was lower than the students belonging to general castes in all DPEP districts except the students of Gajapati district.

Findings Pertaining to the Assessment and Comparison of Learners' Achievement on MAS

1. The average performance of girls over boys belonging to urban area in Language was superior across the DPEP districts, namely, Gajapati, Kalahandi and Rayagada.
2. The average performance of rural girls was invariably less in Language than their urban counterparts.
3. The average performance of rural total group of students was less in two DPEP districts (Bolangir and Dhenkanal) than urban ones. In one district (Rayagada) it was reverse and in the remaining two districts no such differences were observed.
4. There was no such clear gender specific differences in case of SC, in response to Language achievement across districts.

5. Achievement of SC girls belonging to DPEP district was found to be significantly below others including OBC except in the district of Dhenkanal.
6. Average performance of SC boys were significantly inferior to others in two districts (*i.e.*, Dhenkanal and Rayagada).
7. Caste difference in case of Language acquisition does not exist for boys, girls and total groups, so far as SC and others are concerned.
8. Average performance of SC girls in three districts were significantly lower than others in total Language. Similar was the situation in case of ST total vs. others. Only in one district achievement of ST boys were significantly less than others. In all other cases, inter-group differences were not significant.
9. Average performance of SC/ST students in Language barring the district of Dhenkanal, was at the same level as others including OBC. The upper level performance was not quite high.
10. Average performance of both rural and urban SC students exhibit significantly inferior as compared to others in two out of five DPEP districts.
11. In the achievement of Language SC and other (which includes OBC) performed with minor variations in districts.
12. Performance of students of two DPEP districts (*i.e.*, Dhenkanal and Kalahandi) belonging to ST groups were significantly different for rural ST vs. urban ST and total when compared with that of others.
13. In the districts of Dhenkanal and Kalahandi both rural and urban as well as the total group of ST students performed significantly lower in Language than their counterparts.
14. Gender-wise difference did occur in case of both rural and urban sample and their total in two out of five districts.

15. Average performance of boys in each case was higher in mathematics than that of girls, however, in case of Rayagada district, average achievement of urban girls and total girls was higher than their counterparts boys.

16. Gender specific rural urban differences in Mathematics of Class IV was not very clear cut and the trend of difference were mixed up. In case of difference of some districts the rural boys are inferior to urban boys (Dhenkanal); in others the reverse was true (*i.e.*, Bolangir and Kalahandi) where as rural-urban girls comparison has yielded no conclusive inference.

17. In three DPEP districts (*i.e.*, Dhenkanal, Kalahandi and Bolangir) average performance of SC boys was lower than boys belonging to other category, however, in the remaining two districts (*i.e.*, Gajapati and Rayagada) their average performance was higher than their counterparts. The difference was statistically significant.

18. Average performance of SC girls were high in the district of Gajapati, however, in case of Dhenkanal and Kalahandi average performance of SC girls was significantly lower than girls belonging to other castes. In the remaining two districts (*i.e.*, Bolangir and Rayagada) there was no difference.

19. Gender clubbed difference within SC and gender specific difference between SC and other were not established clearly.

20. Average performance of ST boys, ST girls and STs in general are significantly poor than others including OBC.

21. Average performance of ST students was significantly low in the achievement of Mathematics than their respective counterparts in others including OBCs.

22. Average performance of rural SC students in Mathematics belonging to Gajapati and Rayagada districts were superior to others, however, average performance of students belonging to Dhenkanal and Kalahandi were significantly lower than others.

23. The urban SC in two out of five DPEP districts (Bolangir and Dhenkanal) have scored significantly low in the achievement of Mathematics than urban others.

24. Performance of SC in general (Rural and Urban) was significantly inferior to others (Rural and Urban) in the achievement of Mathematics. However, direction of group difference in SC vs. others was district specific.

25. In almost three out of five DPEP districts (Dhenkanal, Kalahandi and Rayagada) DPEP interventions were fruitful in bringing the gap between rural-urban divide, only in one district (Gajapati) average performance of urban students were more in Language than rural students however, the achievement of rural students were higher in language than the urban students belonging to the district of Bolangir.

26. Gender divide did not reflect in achievement difference in language for students of Class IV which was in support of the achievement of the goals of DPEP interventions.

27. In the district of Gajapati, performance of SC students was significantly inferior in Language than others including OBC.

28. Achievement of SC students in Language was superior in two out of five DPEP districts (Dhenkanal and Kalahandi) and in the remaining three districts there was no difference. These findings substantiate the efficacy of DPEP interventions in bridging; the gap as an innovative step towards UEE.

29. Average achievement of Urban students in Class IV was significantly higher on mathematics than the rural counterparts in three DPEP districts (Gajapati, Dhenkanal and Kalahandi). In one district (Bolangir), the rural students were significantly better than urban students and equality was established in other districts. Hence, with increase in educational level, the urban-rural divide was imperative.

30. In the average performance of students belonging to three districts (Bolangir, Gajapati and Kalahandi) in Mathematics, gender difference did not exist.

31. In the district of Dhenkanal boys were significantly superior in the achievement of Mathematics than girls, however, the reverse was true in the district of Rayagada.

32. Average performance of SC students in the achievement of Mathematics in the districts of Bolangir and Dhenkanal was significantly higher than others. However, the reverse was true in the district of Gajapati. There is no significant difference in the achievement of Mathematics in MAS among the students belonging to districts like Kalahandi and Rayagada.

33. ST Students belonging to Bolangir and Rayagada districts were superior to others in mathematics achievement, whereas the reverse was true in the districts of Kalahandi and Gajapati.

Findings Pertaining to Comparative Profiles of Students Achievement on BAS and MAS

1. The average performance of students in language was significantly positive in three out of five DPEP districts (Rayagada) was showing loss of achievement by nearly two per cent, however, in the district of Bolangir, the hike in achievement was twenty percentage points.

2. The average achievement of students belonging to Gajapati district in language was not significant, however, it was significant in the achievement of students belonging to districts like Bolangir, Dhenkanal and Kalahandi. The gain was as much as twenty per cent.

3. Average achievement of students of class I in all districts was significantly positive in Mathematics. The maximum gain was 13 points with minimum gain of 2 points.

4. The average achievement of students in four districts had significant gains in the MAS over the BAS. The

magnitude of this gain was 18 percentage points in Dhenkanal, which was quite high. Only in one district (Rayagada), there was statuesque in Language in the achievement of Language.

5. In the mean percentage of achievement in Mathematics in three out of five districts, namely, Bolangir, Kalahandi and Rayagada, there were significant losses in achievement scores in Mathematics to the extent of three to nine per cent. In the remaining two districts, namely, Gajapati and Dhenkanal there was significant gains which varied from seven to twelve per cent.

Findings Pertaining to the Study and Comparison of the Performance of Learners' Achievement on the Newly Generated Competency-based Achievement Tests in Language (Oriya), Mathematics and EVS at the End of Class III and Class V in DPEP and Non-DPEP districts of Orissa

1. The average performance of the students of Class III of rural girls in Oriya Language belonging to Non-DPEP districts is highest where as the average performance of rural girls of DPEP districts is found at the lower level. However, there is no significant difference in the learners' performance in Oriya language of DPEP and Non-DPEP districts.

2. Learners of Class III belonging to DPEP and Non-DPEP districts occupied similar position in the achievement of Language (Oriya). Significant differences in the mean scores of achievement of Class III students of DPEP and Non-DPEP districts in Oriya Language are noted for different sub groups namely, girls from rural area, SC/ST belonging to rural areas, both boys and girls of rural areas, boys from urban areas, both boys and girls from urban areas, girls from both rural and urban areas, and boys from both rural and urban areas.

3. Achievement of rural girls, rural SC/ST, the rural boys and girls, the boys and girls from both the rural and

urban areas of Non-DPEP districts of Class III is superior Oriya Language than their respective DPEP counterparts. However, Language achievement of Urban and Rural boys, and even both boys and girls from Urban areas of DPEP districts is significantly greater than their respective Non-DPEP counterparts.

4. The learners of Class III of DPEP and Non-DPEP districts vary significantly in the achievement of Mathematics and the difference goes in favour of the learners of Non-DPEP districts.

5. Achievement of learners of Class III of Non-DPEP districts is significantly greater in Mathematics than their DPEP counterparts. Similar is the situation with certain sub-groups.

6. Average performance of the achievement of learners of Class III belonging to Non-DPEP districts is significantly higher in Mathematics than their DPEP counterparts.

7. Performance of the learners of Class III of DPEP districts differs significantly with respect to their achievement in EVS. These differences are in favour of learners of Class III of Non-DPEP districts.

8. Students of Class III belonging to Non-DPEP districts demonstrated significantly positive trends in the achievement of EVS. However, in case of DPEP districts, there is a loss of achievement in EVS by 1.04 per cent, which is significant.

9. Achievement in EVS of learners of Class III in terms of gender, area, and caste of DPEP districts is significantly lower than that of their Non-DPEP counterparts.

10. The learners of Class V of DPEP and Non-DPEP district did not differ significantly with respect to their achievement in Oriya Language. Hence, the learners of Class V belonging to both DPEP and Non-DPEP districts occupied the similar position in the achievement of Oriya

Language. However, in case of DPEP districts, there was a loss of achievement in Oriya Language by 0.32 per cent, which is not significant.

11. Achievement in Oriya Language of the learners of Class V in terms of gender, caste and area of DPEP districts is significantly lower than that of the learners of their Non-DPEP counterparts except boys of DPEP vs. girls of Non-DPEP, and rural boys of DPEP vs. Urban boys of Non-DPEP districts.

12. Average performance of achievement of the boys of Class V belonging to DPEP districts is significantly higher than the girls of Non-DPEP districts, and the achievement of boys of rural DPEP districts is also significantly higher than that of boys of Urban Non-DPEP districts.

13. Learners of Class V of DPEP and Non-DPEP district did not differ significantly in their achievement in Mathematics. Hence, there is no significant difference in Mathematics achievement of learners of Class V of DPEP and Non-DPEP districts. Similar is the situation with certain sub-groups.

14. Achievement of learners of Class V of Non-DPEP districts is significantly higher in Mathematics than their counterparts.

15. The average performance of learners' achievement in EVS of DPEP and Non-DPEP districts of Class V did differ significantly, and the difference goes in favour of the learners of DPEP districts.

16. The achievement of the learners' of Class V of DPEP districts is significantly greater in EVS than their Non-DPEP counterparts.

17. The mean performance of achievement of Class V learners of DPEP and Non-DPEP districts in EVS were exist for different sub-groups, namely, boys from rural areas, girls from rural areas, SC/ST from rural areas,

both boys and girls from rural areas, boys of DPEP and Non-DPEP districts, girls of DPEP and Non-DPEP districts, SC/ST of DPEP and Non-DPEP districts, boys of DPEP district and girls of Non-DPEP districts, rural boys of DPEP districts and Urban boys of Non-DPEP districts, both boys and girls from rural areas of DPEP districts and boys and girls from urban areas of Non-DPEP districts.

18. Rural boys, rural girls, rural SC/ST, rural boys and girls, SC/ST and boys and girls from both rural and urban areas of DPEP districts are superior in the achievement in EVS of Class V than their respective Non-DPEP counterparts.

EDUCATIONAL IMPLICATIONS

The findings of the present study as summarised have implications for planning strategies in general and also district wise, focussing on gender, area and social groups.

One of the objectives of the present study was to examine the impact of DPEP, Orissa on access and retention at the primary stage. For the purpose, a trend analysis has been attempted in terms of different indicators of access and retention as discussed in Chapter II. The analysis, in general, indicates that we are steadily and surely making consistent progress towards the super goals. But our specific observations based on the present study require strategic planning and implementation.

In the DPEP district like Rayagada, the increase in the number of Primary School was not encouraging. So measures need to be taken up to open Primary Schools in such a tribal area. The NFE scheme may continue in some inaccessible areas of Rayagada district. The scheme of Operation Blackboard should be implemented successfully.

Since all sample DPEP districts were found having inadequate essential facilities in the areas of safe drinking water, game equipments, play ground, electric supply, separated toilets for girls, first-aid kids and musical instruments, initiatives may be made to mobilise community members for additional resources in order to ward off the financial crunch and to make available the funds for the above purpose. Thus, a feeling of owning the school on the part of the community will accelerate the process of its greater and genuine participation in the affairs of the school. The VEC/PTA/MTA may be empowered to take the managerial responsibility of primary education at their level. The number of women teachers is relatively small in almost all the DPEP districts. More number of women teachers be appointed and their services could be utilised to rope in non-enrolled children and retaining those who are enrolled. What is needed a large number of teachers from SC and ST Communities. Steps may be taken to appoint more qualified teachers in the remote areas of these DPEP districts. More professionally qualified teachers be appointed in different Primary Schools of these districts.

Removal of gender disparities in access and retention is a key objective of DPEP. The findings show that there has been an increase in girls' enrolment in all the project districts (except Dhenkanal and Rayagada for Class III). This is a very positive development that indicates that increase in enrolment in DPEP districts has been more for girls than the boys. But a sorry state of affairs, so far as girls' enrolment is concerned, is noted in case of Dhenkanal and Rayagada districts. Hence more focussed attention is required to improve girls' participation in the DPEP districts like Dhenkanal and Rayagada. More number of women teachers are to be appointed in these two DPEP districts to tackle the problem of girls' participation. It is also evident that DPEP interventions have resulted in considerable gains in enrolment of the SC and ST population. But there is scope for improving the enrolment of ST children in some of the DPEP districts, especially in Kandhamala, Rayagada and Bolangir. It can also be noted that in the district like Dhenkanal the rate of girls' drop-out is high. The following intervention strategies have been proposed for the purpose.

Parental awareness towards primary education of their children should be increased.

- Physical access through opening of school and providing teachers and constructing buildings be provided.
- Alternative School in small habitations where formal school is not viable be provided.
- Management of Primary education should be in the hands of community.
- Incentives/scholarships among ST students should be taken up in a large scale.
- Residential schools, including Ashram Schools be provided in a large scale.
- Curriculum be designed to create an awareness of the rich cultural identity of the tribal people as also of their enormous creative talent.
- Educated and promising SC/ST youth be encouraged to take up teaching in tribal areas after due training.
- Instructional materials be developed in tribal languages at the initial stages, with arrangements for switching over to the regional language.
- In service teachers training programme on MLL, joyful Learning should be planned and capacity building at different levels be emphasised.
- Door-to-Door survey be taken up to enrol girls and SC and ST children.
- Activity based instruction be encouraged.
- Mid-day meal programme be continued, enriched and ensured.
- Contracts with parents about the progress of the child be assured.

Findings relating to BAS indicate clearly inter district disparity in school achievement in Oriya language and numeracy of Class II children. Significant gender difference in both language and numeracy achievement did occur in Bolangir district favouring boys over girls. Urban student were found to be superior than the rural students (Class-II) in their language and numeracy achievement. Significant difference in language did occur favouring Non SC/ST students. Significant caste difference in numeracy did occur only in Gajapati district favouring non SC/ST students. These findings do suggest that there is need to understand not these demographic factors alone or in isolation but classroom dynamics as well so that during teaching focus be centred around girls, SC, ST and rural children relatively a little more. This brings into focus a planning strategy in DPEP that teachers be oriented, monitored as well as academically supervised during teaching by necessary supervisory functionaries for on spot remedy of the situation, rather than routine in-service training which are going on in the education without follow up mechanism since inception. The above observations, generalisation and implications are also applicable for numeracy achievement of students in class II. This strategy will eventually level up the inter-district disparity, whatever exists either due to real ecological factor, instructional deficiency, test artifact or from within organisational mechanism.

Findings pertaining to MAS indicate no difference in respect of gender divide, rural-urban divide and social groups. This suggests that DPEP intervention has made a significant impact.

Dhenkanal and Kalahandi Districts have taken greater advantage of this intervention than other districts. In fact, in 16 cases of inter-group comparisons, results of DPEP interventions are encouraging in reducing gaps but level of achievement is not very high.

These call for attention to plan out effective monitoring, supervision as well as follow-up system. But at the same time equipping teachers with language and reading skills with illustration, exercise and specified techniques. There is sufficient back up evidences in the literature and researches on language learning (Patnayak , 1992; Panda, 1999) based on Benstein's (1962) model as well as Laddo's (1964) language learning and teaching. Quality what is what one needs in intervention not merely a spurt.

Gender specific rural urban divide analysis established equity than difference in mathematics achievement. The same is true for SC group when compared with others with reference to gender groups. In the case of ST children, lower performance in mathematics achievement was indicated. One generalisation can be made that gaps in mathematics achievement among various comparison groups on the basis of gender, area and social groups have been reduced to minimum which is a plus for DPEP intervention but at the same time one could also say that the restricted range of achievement in mathematics has made the inter-group differences less sensitive. In any case, by following up the inputs into the primary school we can strengthen the efficacy of DPEP intervention and stabilize whatever positives have been achieved.

In all such cases, the districts of Dhenkanal and Kalahandi appear as major beneficiary of the intervention. Hence, while following up not only more stress is needed for the other districts but more is to find if, there is any indigenous practice with teachers of Dhenkanal and Kalahandi. DPEP schools leading to such success, and if so, the success stories can be shared by others through the mechanism of DPEP.

In case of most or all districts significant achievement gains were seen from initial survey to MAS for class I students. In language it was up to 20 per cent rise and for mathematics it was 13 points rise. In class IV, Language achievement gains were significantly noticeable in four (Bolangir, Dhenkanal, Gajapati and Kalahandi) out of five districts. On the contrary in two districts (Dhenkanal and Gajapati) mathematics achievement noticed significant gains but in three districts (Bolangir, Kalahandi and Rayagada) there was loss which was also significant. While it can be easily construed as a direct benefit of the DPEP intervention through qualitative changes brought in teaching learning process, the losses in achievement in mathematics could most probably be due to a less appropriate test measuring mathematics achievement. Hence, DPEP authorities, entrusted with test development may look at revision of the test in further study. Specific attention needs be given to the three districts where there is loss by making an assessment of intervening variables between initial and MAS test. This is the overall scene.

The question is, about gender variation in achievement gains. Girls and boys of Class I in three district (Bolangir, Dhenkanal and Gajapati) districts maintained significant gains in language achievement. Both boys and girls had significant gain in mathematics achievement in almost all districts. The girls have gained more points than boys in both language and mathematics. In case of boys and girls of class IV gains were seen in language and mathematics in the same three districts (Bolangir, Dhenkanal and Gajapati) and losses in Kalahandi and Rayagada which are predominantly tribal.

While establishing the validity of DPEP intervention, the findings suggest that as children move from early grades to upper classes in primary schools of Kalahandi and Rayagada districts. Probably a more direct control, continuous monitoring and follow up is necessary even upto class IV. May be there is a need of introspection from within the establishment in these two districts, which will explain the facts better, leading district specific attention based on internal dynamics.

The observations regarding the pre-eminence of the element of contextuality during the MAS has also been confirmed through the findings of the present study by way of comparing the learners of DPEP and non-DPEP districts on their achievement (*i.e.*, Mathematics, Language and EVS) on the newly generated competency based tests. For instance, significant achievement gains in EVS has been noticed in case of DPEP districts for Class V students. There are ample evidences of wide inter-group variations across the districts. These suggest that DPEP intervention has made a mixed impact on the contrary, significant losses can be observed in the achievement of mathematics and EVS for class III students. All these obviously warrant district specific educational plans and varied interventions for individual districts to cater to their specific needs.

SUGGESTIONS FOR FURTHER RESEARCH

In the light of present study the following suggestions are offered for further research:

(i) This study may be replicated on lager samples covering other DPEP districts of Orissa.

(ii) Home-related and school-related factors may be studies in relation to learners' achievement.

(iii) Refinement of competency-based achievement tests in Oriya language, mathematics and EVS may be attempted in most precise manner.

(iv) The statistical techniques like ANOVA and ANCOVA may be used for better analysis of data.

(v) The findings of the study need further cross validation.

BIBLIOGRAPHY

Agarwal, S. and Harding, D. (1995). A Community-based Effort in Enhancing School Effectiveness and Learning Achievement : A Case Study from Ghana. In K. Kumar (Ed.) *School Effectiveness and Learning Achievement at Primary Stage : International Perspective*; New Delhi : N.C.E.R.T., 291-308.

Aggarwal, Y. (1999). A Comparative Analysis of Access and Retention in DPEP District and Non-DPEP. Districts : In J.P. Sharma (Ed). *Research in School Effectiveness at Primary Stage*, New Delhi: N.C.E.R.T., 6-7.

Aggarwal, Y. (1999). *Trends in Access and Retention : A Study of Primary Schools in DPEP Districts*, New Delhi: Ed. CIL.

Aggarwal, Y. (2000). Access and Retention. *DPEP Calling* 6(11), 36-48.

Aggarwal, Y. (2000). Which Districts Benefited the Most from *DPEP?DPEP Calling*, 6(10),5-9.

Alexander, R.J. (1992). *Policy and Practice in Primary Education*. London : Routledge.

Alexander, R.J. (1995). *Versions of Primary Education*. London : Routledge.

Alexander, R.J. (1996). *Other Primary School and Ours : Hazards of International Comparison* Warwick : Centre for Research in Elementary and Primary Education.

Ambasht, N.K. and Rath, K.B. (1995). A Study of the Effect of Household, Community and School Factors on the Enrolment,

Retention and Achievement of Scheduled Tribe Children at Primary Level *Indian Educational Review*, 30(1), 123-174.

Anderson, L. and Burns, R. (1989). *Research in Classrooms: The Study of Teachers, Teaching and Instructions*, Oxford, England : Pergamon.

Andreas, P. (1996). Progressive and Alternative Schools as Stimuli for Established School System. *Education*, 54, 38-46.

Armitage, J. *et al.*, (1986). *School Quality and Achievement in Rural Brazil* (Discussion Paper Series No. EDT-25). Washington, D.C : World Bank.

Asthana, M. (1993). A Study of Socio-Psychological Correlates of Dropouts of Senior Basic Level. Ph.D., Edu. Rohilkand University. *Indian Educational Abstract*, 6, 11.

Barpanda, N. (1997). Teacher Empowerment Strategies to Ensure Community Involvement in UEE : A Case Study of Tribal Areas of Sambalpur District. *Indian Educational Abstract* 6, 11.

Behera, K. and Das, G. (1999). Effects of Learning Corner Activities on Learner's Achievement in J.P. Sharma (Ed). *Research in School Effectiveness at Primary Stage*. New Delhi :N.C.E.R.T., 12-13.

Bennett, S.N. *et al.*, (1984). *The Quality of Pupil Learning Experiences*. Hove: Lawrence Eribaum.

Bert, P.M. *et al.*, (1996). Educational Effectiveness for Different Student Groups. In K. Kumar (Ed.). *School Effectiveness and Learning Achievement at Primary Stage* : International Perspective, New Delhi: N.C.E.R.T., 109-140.

Best, J.W. (1978). *Research in Education*. New Delhi: Prentice Hall of India Pvt. Ltd.

Boneau, C.A. (1960). The Effects of Violation of Assumption Underlying the 't' test. *Psychological Bulletin*, 1 (XII), 62.

Bosker, R.J. and Scheerens, J. (1989). Issues in the Interpretation of the Results of School Effectiveness Research. *International Journal of Education Research*, 13, 741-752.

Buch, M.B. (ed.) (1997). *Fifth Survey of Research in Education* (1988-92). New Delhi : N.C.E.R.T.

Carew, J. and Light Foot, S. (1979). *Beyond Bias : Perspective on Classroom*. Cambridge, MA : Harvard University Press.

Chakrabarti, S. (1999). Non-Detention Pand Drop-out in Primary Education. *Indian Educational Abstract*, 6,12.

Chan, C.C. *et al.*, (1992). Primary School Teacher Self Concept : Its Relationship with Teacher Behaviours and Students' Educational Outcomes. *Primary Education*. 3(1), 9-28. The Chinese University of Hong Kong.

Chapman, D.W. (1993). *Improving the Effectiveness and Efficiency of Schooling : What have We Learned from Eight Years of IEES Research* Improving the Efficiency of Education Systems (IEES) Project. Learning Systems Institute. Tallahassee : Florida State University.

Chapman, E.W. (1995). Improving Instructional Practice : The teachers' dilemma. In K. Kumar (Ed.). *School Effectiveness and Learning Achievement at Primary Stage : International Prospective*; New Delhi: N.C.E.R.T., 325-344.

Chatterjee, B. (1997). Primary Education : The Indian Experience. *DPEP Calling*, 1(14), 25-33.

Cheng, Y.C. (1991 a). Function and Effectiveness of Education. Hong Kong : Wide Angle Press, 428.

Cheng, Y.C. (1994). Classroom Environment and Students' Affective Performance : An Effective Profile : *Journal of Experimental Education* 62(3), 221-231.

Cheng, Y.C. (1996). Effective Classroom Environment for Student's Satisfaction and Academic Achievement. In R.S. Saxena (Ed.) *Studies on Classroom Processes and School Effectiveness at Primary Stage*. New Delhi: N.C.E.R.T., 27-42.

Cohen, D. (1990). A Revolution in One Classroom : The Case of Mrs. Oublier. Educational *Evaluation and Policy Analysis* 12, 311-329.

Cohen. D. and Spllane, J. (1992). Policy and Practice. The Relation Between Governance and Instruction. In G. Grant.

(Ed.) *Review of Research in Education*, 3-49. Washington, DC : AERA.

Creemers, B.P.M. (1992). School Effectiveness and Effective Instruction : The need for a Further Relationship. In J. Bashi and Z. Sass (Eds.) *School Effectiveness and Improvement*. Proceedings of the Third International Congress, 105-132. Jerusalem : The Magnes Press.

Creemers, B.P.M. (1994). *The Effective Classroom*. London : Cassell.

Creemers, B.P.M. (1995). Educational Effectiveness for Different Student Groups. In K. Kumar (Ed.) *School Effectiveness and Learning Achievement at Primary Stage : International Prospective*, New Delhi: N.C.E.R.T., 109-142.

Creemers, B.P.M. *et al.*, (1996). *World Class Schools : Some Further Findings*. Paper Presented at the Annual Conference of the American Educational Research Association, New York.

Dalin, P. (1994). How School Improve : *An International Report*, London : Cassell.

Dave, P.N. *et al.*, (1988). *Pupil Achievement at the Primary Stage*. Department of Pre-school and Elementary Education, New Delhi: N.C.E.R.T.

Dave, P.N. *et al.*, (1988). Achievement Under Project PECR (Mimeographed), New Delhi : N.C.E.R.T.

Department of Education (1995). *District Primary Education Programme Guidelines*. Ministry of Human Resource Development, New Delhi.

Dorasoami, K. *et al.*, (1999). Enhancement of Learning Achievement in Mathematics through Empowerment of Teacher Competence : an Experiment : In J.P. Sharma (Ed.). *Research in School Effectiveness at Primary Stage*. New Delhi : N.C.E.R.T., 24-25.

DPEP (1995). *State Component Plan*. KGPSM. Bhopal, 64-79.

Dreeben, R. (1968). *On What is Learned in School*. Reading, MA : Addision Wesley.

Duhan, K. *et al.*, (1997). Language Performance Among Pre-Schoolers. *Indian Educational Abstract*, 5, 25-26.

Easwari, P. (1996). Set Backs in UEE/Primary Education in India. *DPEP Calling*, 1(3), 33-37.

Elley, W. (1992). *How in the World do Sstudents Read*? The Hague, Netherlands : I E A.

Fraser, B.J. and Fisher, D.L. (1982). Predicting Student's Outcomes from Their Perception of Classroom Psychosocial Environment. *American Education Research Journal* 19, 498-518.

Fuller, B. (1987). What School Factors Raise Achievement in the Third World? *Review of Educational Research*. 57 (3), 255-292.

Fuller, B. and Heyneman, S. (1989). Third World School Quality : Current Collapse Future Potential *Educational Research*. 18(2), 12-19.

Fuller, B. and Clarke, P. (1996). Life in Indian Classroom : The Influence of Culture and Caste. In R.S. Saxena (Ed.). *Studies on Classroom Processes and School Effectiveness at Primary Stage*, New Delhi: N.C.E.R.T., 329-259.

Gamoran, A. (1986). Instructional and Institutional Effects of Ability Grouping. *Sociology of Education*. 59, 185-198.

Garrett, H.E. (1981). *Statistics in Psychology and Education*. Bombay : Vakils Feffer and Simons.

Goel, S.K. (1996). A Study of Mathematical Language Needs of Student's of Class I and II for Smooth Transaction from Concrete to Abstract Stages of Comprehension of Mathematics Teaching. *Indian Educational Abstract*, 5, 44-45.

Goel, S.K. (1996). Identification of Learning Problems in Arithmetic and Remedial Teaching for Children in Standard I. In R.S. Saxena (Ed.) *Studies on Classroom Processes and School Effectiveness at Primary Stage*. New Delhi : N.C.E.R.T., 292-309.

Good, T.L. and Brophy, J.E. (1986). School Effects. In M.C. Wittrock (Ed.) *Hand Book of Research on Teaching*. (3rd ed.). New York : Macmillan, 370-602.

Goodlad, J. (1984). *A Place Called School.* New York : McGraw-Hill.

Government of India (1992). *National Policy on Education, 1986* : Programme of Action, 1992. M.H.R.D. (Department of Education), New Delhi.

Govinda, K. and Varghese, N.V. (1992). Quality of Primary Education : An Empirical Study, *Journal of Educational Planning and Administration*, 6(1), 17-35.

Grover, I. (1988). *Universalisation Primary Education as Innovation : A Study of Wastage in an Indian Village.* DEE. HALL Press, Hissar.

Gupta, J.K. and Gupta, M.K. (1995). Effect of State Interventions on Pupil's Achievement. *Indian Educational Review*, 30(1), 71-85.

Gupta, V.P. *et al.*, (1999). Learning Achievement of Children Studying in Alternative Schools of DPEP Districts of Madhya Pradesh. *Indian Educational Review*, 35(2), 135-154.

Hadges, L. *et al.*, (1993). *A Meta Analysis of Studies of the Effects of Differential Schools Expenditures on Student Outcomes*: Chicago : University of Chicago.

Hanushek, E. (1981). Throwing Money at Schools. *Journal of Policy Analysis and Management*, 1(1), 19-41.

Hanushek, E. (1986). The Economics of Schooling : Production and Efficiency in Public Schools, *Journal of Economic Literature*, 24, 1141-1177.

Heneveld, W. (1994). Planning and Monitoring the Quality of Primary Education in Sub-Saharan Africa. *Technical Note No. 14*, Human Resources and Poverty Division, Technical Department, Africa Region, Washington, D.C : The World Bank.

Heyneman, S. (1976). Influences on Academic Achievement. A Comparison of Results from Uganda and More Industrialised Societies. *Sociology of Education*, 49, 200-201.

Heyneman, S. P. and Loxley, W. A. (1983). The Effect of Primary School Quality on Academic Achievement Across 29 High and Low Income Countries. *American Journal of Sociology*, 88(6), 1162-1194.

Hillway, T. (1956). *Introduction to Research.* Boston : Houghton Mifflin.

Holloway, S. *et al.,* (1990). The Family's Influence an Achievement in Japan and the United Slates. *Comparative Education Review,* 34(20); 196-208.

Hussain, A. (1997). An unfinished Agenda. DPEP Calling, 1(14), 34-46.

Jain, V. K. (1995). Effect of School Policies and Practices on Students Achievement. In K. Kumar (Ed.) *School Effectiveness and learning Achievement at Primary Stage: International Perspective,* N.C.E.R.T., 43-168.

Jain, V.K. and Arora, O. P. (1995). Effect of School Level Variables on Achievement Gap Between Boys and Girls. *Indian Educational Review,* 30(1), 26-51.

Jangaiah, C. (1998). Learning Styles of Primary School Children. *Indian Educational Abstract,* 6, 15.

Jangira, N. K. (1994). *Learning Achievement of Primary School Children in Reading and Mathematics in Research Based Interventions in Primary Education. The DPEP Strategy* : New Delhi: N.C.E.R.T.

Jangira, N. K. and Ahuja, A. (1995). *Learning Achievement of Children at Primary Level. A Baseline Assessment study of four Districts of Haryana.* Department of Teacher Education and Special Education, New Delhi: N.C.E.R.T.

Jangira, N. K. and Paranjpe, S. (1995). *Learning Achievement of Children at Primary Level, A Base Line Assessment Study in Three Districts of Maharashtra.* Department of Teacher Education and Special Education, New Delhi: N.C.E.R.T.

Jangira, N. K. and Rath, K. B. (1995). Input in Primary Schools with Different Levels of Concentration of Scheduled Tribe Students. *Indian Educational Review.,* 30 (1), 86-112.

Jena, S. L. and Mohanty, M. M. (1996). *School Effectiveness and Learner Achievement: A Baseline Assessment Study of Primary Schools in Orissa,* Bhubaneswar, Directorate of T.E.

and S.C.E.R.T., Department of School and Mass Education. Government of Orissa.

Jena, S. L. and Mohanty, M. M. (1997). *School Effectiveness and Learner Achievement: A Baseline Assessment Study of Primary Schools in Orissa*, Bhubaneswar, Directorate, T.E. and S.C.E.R.T., Department of School and Mass Education, Government of Orissa.

Johnson, R. (1992). *Factors Relating to Students Achievement*. Washington, D.C.: Bureau for Research and Development, Office of Education.

Juneja, N. (1997). Compulsory Education : A Path Analysis. *DPEP Calling*, 1(15), 24-40.

Kamat, K. (1999). Programme for Upgradation of Achievement of Children Studying in Grade I to IV of Municipal Primary Schools (Marathi Medium) 'S' ward, Mumbai by empowering teachers. *Indian Educational Abstract*, 6, 15.

Kapoor, R. *et al.*, (1996). Numeracy and Reading Readiness Levels of Entrants to Class I. In R.S. Saxena (Ed.) *Studies on Classroom Processes and School Effectiveness at Primary Stage*. New Delhi: N.C.E.R.T., 715-738.

Khader, M. A. (1996). Empowering Primary Teachers for Effective Classroom Transactions in PREP Schools. *Indian Educational Abstract*, 5, 29.

Kularatna, N. G. (1999). Project for Improvement of Education in Small Deprived Primary Schools in Sri Lanka, in V. Prakash (Ed.) *Research in school Effectiveness of Primary Stage*, New Delhi: N.C.E.R.T., 11-12.

Kulkarni, S. S. (1970). *All India Survey of Achievement in Mathematics*, New Delhi : N.C.E.R.T.

Lakshmi, K. (1996). Impact of School Readiness Programme on Primary School Children. In R.S. Saxena (Ed.) *Studies on Classroom Processes and School Effectiveness at Primary Stage*. New Delhi : N.C.E.R.T., 555-568.

Lakshmi Naraya, U. *et al.*, (1999). Motivation and Classroom Practices as Indicators of School Effectiveness: In J.P. Sharma

(Ed.) *Research in School Effectiveness at Primary Stage*, New Delhi: N.C.E.R.T., 19-20.

Levin, H. and Marlaine, E. L. (Eds.), (1989). *Effective Schools in Developing Countries*. Washington, D.C : Falmer Press.

Levine, D. U. and Lezotte, L. W. (1990). Usually Effective Schools : *A review and Analysis of Research and Practice*. Madison : National Centre for Effective School Research and Development.

Levine, R. *et al.*, (1991). *Learning in Developing Countries : Reconceptualising the Educational Process*. Unpublished Manuscript. UNESCO.

Lockheed, M. and Komenan, A. (1989). Teaching Quality and Student Achievement in Africa : The Case of Nigeria and Switzerland. *Teaching and Teacher Education*, 5(2), 93-113.

Lockheed, M. *et al.*, (1989). Family Effects on Students' Achievement in Thailand and Malawi, *Sociology of Education*, 62, 239-256.

Lockheed, M. *et al.*, (1991). *Improving Primary Education in Developing Countries*. London : Oxford University Press.

Lockheed, M. E. and Adriaan, M. V. (1991). *Improving Primary Education in Developing Countries*. Oxford : Oxford University Press.

Lockheed. M. E. and Verspoor, A. M. (1991). *Improving Primary Education in Developing countries*. Washington : World Bank in Conjunction with Oxford University Press.

Mehan, H. (1992). Understanding Inequality in Schools; The Contribution of Interpretive Studies. *Sociology of Education*, 65, 1-20.

Mohapatro, M. (1999). Identification of Misconceptions Related to Astronomical Beliefs at Primary Stage and Intervention Strategies : A March Towards school Effectiveness. In J. P. Sharma (Ed.) *Research in School Effectiveness at Primary Stage*, New Delhi: N.C.E.R.T., 15-16.

Mouly, G. J. (1964). *The Science of Educational Research*. New Delhi : Eurasia Publishing House Pvt. Ltd.

Mphuthi, T. and Adeola, 0. A. (1998). Learning Organisation and the Effectiveness of Primary Education in Lesotho : A Case Atudy of Roma Valley Primary Schools. In V. Prakash (Ed.) *Studies on Learning Organisation, Community Participation and School Effectiveness at Primary Stage*, New Delhi : N.C.E.R.T., 356-368.

Murnane, R. J. (1981). Interpreting the Evidence on School Effectiveness. *Teachers College Record*, 1983, 19-35.

Mwamwenda, T. and Mwamwenda, B. (1987). School Facilities and Pupils' Academic Achievement. *Comparative Education Review*, 23(2), 225-235.

Nagaraju, C. S. (1995). Intervention for MLL Attainment in Multigrade Contexts. In K. Kumar (Ed.) *School Effectiveness and Learning Achievement at Primary Stage* : International Perspective, New Delhi : N.C.E.R.T., 471-480,

Nagpal, S. (1995). *Learning Achievement of Primary School Children in Reading and Mathematics in Orissa*, New Delhi: N.C.E.R.T.

Naik, J. P. (1975). *Elementary Education in India : A Promise to Keep*. Bomleary : Allied Publication Pvt. Ltd.

Nair, P.V. (1999). A Comparative Study of Classroom Climate in DPEP and NON-DPEP Schools of Kerala. In J.P. Sharma (Ed.) *Research on School Effectiveness at Primary Stage*, New Delhi: N.C.E.R.T., 21-22.

Nayar, U. (1995). Gender Issues Primary Education. *Indian Educational Review*, 30 (1), 220-245.

Nayar, U. (1995). Planning for UPE of Girls and Women's Empowerment. Gender studies in DPEP. K. Kumar (Ed.) *School Effectiveness and Learning Achievement at Primary Stage*, International Perspective, New Delhi: N.C.E.R.T., 579-610.

N.C.E.R.T. (1991). *Minimum Levels of Learning at Primary Stage*. Report of the Committee set up by MHRD, Govt. of India, New Delhi.

N.C.E.R.T. (1994). *Research Based Intervention in Primary Education : DPEP Strategy*, New Delhi: N.C.E.R.T

National Council of Education Research and Training. (1995). *School Effectiveness and Learning Achievement at Primary Stage*. New Delhi: N.C.E.R.T.

Pradhan, N. (1996). Minimum Level of Learning in Mathematics for Class III Children in Orissa. *Indian Educational Review*, 35(1), 117-122.

Prakash, V. and Panda, P. (1996). Literacy and Numeracy Attainment of Class II Students in DPEP States- A Meta Analysis. In R.S. Saxena (Ed.) *Studies on Classroom Processes and School Effectiveness at Primary Stage*. New Delhi: N.C.E.R.T., 337-346.

Prakash, V. and Pandey, S. (1996). Influence of Demographic Variables on Learners, Achievement *Indian Educational Review*, 31(1), 36-46.

Padhi, J.S. (1996). Effect of Competency Based Activity-Centred Approach to Teaching on Attainment of Mastery Level Learning in Environmental Studies. In R.S. Saxena (Ed.) *Studies on Classroom Process and School Effectiveness at Primary Stage*. New Delhi : N.C.E.R.T., 321-327.

Padhi, J.S. *et al.*, (1997). Effect of School Climate Indicators on Learners' Achievement at Primary Stage : Teacher Empowerment Issues. In V. Prakash (Ed.) *Teacher Empowerment and School Effectiveness at Primary Stage*, New Delhi: N.C.E.R.T., 167-174.

Panda, B.N. (2001). Indicators of Quality Learning Achievement of Primary School Children of Orissa. *The Primary Teacher*, XXVI (I), 30-41.

Prakash, V. *et al.*, (1999). An Appraisal of Students' Achievement during Mid-Term Assessment Survey Under DPEP. In J.P. Sharma (Ed.) *Research in School Effectiveness at Primary Stage*. New Delhi: N.C.E.R.T., 8-9.

Panda, K.C. and Jena, S.L. (1999). *School Effectiveness and Learner Achievement: A Mid-Term Assessment Survey in Orrisa*, Bhubaneswar, Directorate of T.E. and S.C.E.R.T., Department of School and Mass Education, Government of Orissa.

Panda, S.C. (1996). Effect of Competency-based Instruction in Achieving MLL Competencies in Grade IV in Oriya Medium Schools. In R.S. Saxena (Ed.) *Studies Classroom Processes and School Effectiveness at Primary Stage.* New Delhi: N.C.E.R.T., 653-667.

Pandey R.S. (1998). Four Years of DPEP—The Challenges Ahead *DPEP Calling.* III (1),1-17.

Purkey, S.C. and Marshall, S.S. (1983). Effective Schools; A Review. *Elementary School Journal.* 83(4), 427-452.

Purkey, W. W. (1970). *Self Concept and School Achievement.* Englewood Cliff, NJ. Prentice-Hall.

Rajakutty, S. (1995), A Case of Operation Black-Board Programme in India, in R. R. Saxena (Ed.) *Studies on Classroom Processes and School Effectiveness at Primary Stage.* New Delhi: N.C.E.R.T.

Ramachandran, V.K. *et al.,* (1997). Investment Gaps in Primary Education. *DPEP Calling,* 1 (11), 7-21

Rath K.B. and Saxena, R.R. (1995). Effect of Pupil and School Level Variables on the Achievement of Schedule Caste/ Schedule Tribe Students. *Indian Educational Review,* 30(1), 52-70.

Rath, K.B. *et al.,* (1996). .Effect of Schooling Process on Learning Outcome. *Indian Educational Abstract,* 5, 31-32.

Raudenbush, S. and Willms, J. (Eds.) (1991). *School, Classrooms and Pupils: International Studies of Schooling from a Multilevel Perspective.* San Diego: Academic.

Ray, J. (1996). Class Room Reorganisation : A Challenge for Universal Retention of Females. In R.R Saxena (Ed.) *Studies on Classroom Processes and School Effectiveness at Primary Stage,* New Delhi : N.C.E.R.T.

Reddy, V.E. (1995). Primary Education in the Web of Poverty Culture. In K. Kumar (Ed.) *School Effectiveness and Learning Achievement at Primary Stage*: International Perspective. New Delhi: N.C.E.R.T., 253-258.

Reimers, F. (1992). *Influence on Student Achievement in Pakistan*. Paper presented at the BIRDGES/IEES Conference on schooling Effectiveness. Harvard institute for International Development, Cambridge M.A.

Reynolds, D. (1993). Linking School Effectiveness Knowledge and School Improvement Practice. In Dimmock (Ed.) *School Based Management and School Effectiveness*, London : Routledge, 185-200.

Reynolds, D. and Teddlie, C. (1995). *World Class Schools: A Preliminary Analysis from the International School Effectiveness Research Project* (ISERP). New Castle Upon Tyne : University of New Castle Upon Tyne.

Riddell, A.R. (1995). School Effectiveness and School Improvement in the Third World : A Stock-Taking and Implications for the Development of Indicators. In K. Kumar (Ed.) *School Effectiveness and Learning Achievement at Primary Stage: International Perspective*, New Delhi: N.C.E.R.T., 49-76.

Ross, K.N. and PostLethwaite, T.N. (1992). Indicators of the Quality of Education : A Summary of a National Study of Primary Schools in Zimbabwe, *IIEP Research Report*, No. 96, Paris: IIEP.

Rowe, K.J. *et al.*, (1994). *Assessing, Recording and* Reporting Students' Educational Progress : The Case for Profiles. Paper for the 1994 Conference of the Australian Association for Research in Education.

Roy, S.G. *et al.*, (1995). Evaluation of Attainment Level of Primary Students: The West Bengal Example. In K. Kumar (Ed.). *School Effectiveness and Learning Achievement at Primary Stage*. New Delhi : N.C.E.R.T., 399-404.

Rutter, M. (1983). School effects on Pupil Progress : Research Findings and Policy Implications. *Child Development*, 54(1), 1-29.

Sammons, P. *et al.*, (1995). *Key Characteristics of Effective Schools : A Review of School Effectiveness Research*. London : OFSTED.

Saxena, R.R. *et al.*, (1995). *School Effectiveness and Learners Achievement at Primary Stage*. New Delhi : N.C.E.R.T.

Scheerens, J. (1992). *Effective Schooling : Research, Theory and Practice*. London : Cassell.

Schiefelvein, E. and Simmons, J. (1981). *The Determinants of School Achievement: A Review of the Research for Developing Countries*. Ottawa: IDRC.

Senapathy, J.K. (1995). Universalisation of Primary Education and Equity in Quality. In R.S. Saxena (Ed.) *Studies on Classroom Processes and School Effectiveness at Primary Stage*, New Delhi : N.C.E.R.T., 482-495.

Serpell, R. (1993). *The Significance of Schooling : Life-Tourney in an African Society*. Cambridge : Cambridge University Press.

Sharma, R. *et al.*, (1998). Functioning of Alternative Schools on DPEP Districts of Madhya Pradesh. In V. Prakash (Ed.) *Studies on Learning Organisation and Community Participation and School Effectiveness at Primary Stage*, New Delhi: N.C.E.R.T., 130-140.

Shukla, S. (1994). *Attainment of Primary School Children in Various States*. New Delhi : N.C.E.R.T.

Shukla, N. (1995). Effectiveness of Various Interventions for Improving Tribal Education. *Indian Educational Review*, 30(1), 175-189.

Singh,, J. *et al.*, (1989). *Socio-Economic Environment, Academic Achievement and Occupation Opportunities in Malaysia*. Executive Summary Presited to the Ministry of Education, Educational Planning and Research Division, Kualalumpur, Malaysia.

Singh, N. and Bala. S.(1996), Study of Role Perception of VEC Members of DPEP District in Haryana. *Indian Educational Abstract*. 5,1-2.

Singh, S. and Saxena, R.R. (1995). Achievement Difference and School Effects. *Indian Educational Review*, 30(1), 1-25.

Singh, S. (1996). Determinants of Learner Achievement at Primary Stage. *Indian Educational Review*, 31(1), 47-68.

Slavin, R.E. (1996). Education for all : Research and Reform Towards the Success for all Children. In R.E. Slavin (Ed.) *Education for All*, Lisse : Swets and Zeitlinger, 1-13.

Srivastava, A. B.L. (1999). Internal Efficiency of Primary Education in Phase-I DPEP Districts. In J.P. Sharma (Ed.) *Research in School Effectiveness at Primary Stage*. New Delhi: N.C.E.R.T., 7-8.

Srivastava, G. (1996). Parents and Teachers Perceptions of Gender Related Issues for Improving Access, Enrolment, Retention and Achievement of Girls at Primary Stage. In R. S. Saxena (Ed.) *Studies on Classroom Processes and School Effectiveness at Primary Stage*. New Delhi: N.C.E.R.T., 739-755.

Srivastava, G.N.P. (1996). Study of DPEP Teachers Training Programme- MP and Maharashtra. *Indian Educational Abstract* 5, 58-59.

Stephens, D. (1990). Qualitative Factors in Education, Research and Development : A Position Paper. *International Journal of Educational Development*, 10(23), 143-149.

Stringfield, S.C. and Slavin, R.E. (1992). A Hierarchical Longitudinal Model for Elementary School Effects. In B.P.M. Creemers and G.J. Reezigt (Eds.) *Evaluation of Education Effectiveness*. Groningen : ICO, 35-69.

Stringfield, S.C. (1994). A Model of Elementary School Effects. In D. Reynolds *et al.*, (Eds.) *Advances in School Effectiveness Research and Practice*. Oxford : Porgamon, 153-189.

Sunwani, V.K. and Das, P.K. (1998). Role of the NGO in UEE. A Case Study of GRAGAMME. In V. Prakash (Ed.) *Studies on Learning Organisation, Community Participation and School Effectiveness at Primary Stage*. New Delhi: N.C.E.R.T., 269-276.

Teddlie, C. (1994). The Study of Context in School Effects research : History, Methods, Results and Theoretical

Implications. In P. S. Creemers *et al.*, (Eds.) *Advances in School Effectiveness Research and Practice*. Oxford : Pergamon, 85-111.

Tenner, A.R. and Detoro, I.J. (1992). Total Quality Management. M.A.: Addison-Wesley Publishing Co. Ltd.

Tiguryera, S. (1999). School Effectiveness at Primary Stage : A View of Kampala School Improvement Project. In V. Prakash (Ed.) *Research in School Effectiveness at Primary Stage*. New Delhi: N.C.E.R.T., 10-11.

Tilak, J.B.G. (1997). Investment Gaps. *DPEP Calling*, 1(15), 41-47.

Trickett, E.J. (1978). Towards a Social-Ecological Conception of Adolescent Types of CXW32 Public School Classrooms. *Child Development* 49, 408-414.

Varghese, N.V. (1995). School Effects on Achievement : A Study of Government and Private Aided Schools in Kerala. In K. Kumar (Ed.) *School Effectiveness and Learning Achievement at Primary Stage : International Perspective*, New Delhi: N.C.E.R.T., 216-288.

Varghese, W.V. (1995). *The Case of DPEP*. Paper of Oxford International Conference on Globalisation and Learning, 21-25 September, Oxford.

Velez, E. *et al.*, (1993). *Factors Affecting Achievement in Primary School* (Staff Working Paper/Mimeo). Washington, DC : World Bank.

Waxman, H.C. *et al.*, (1992). Investigating the Effects of Classroom Learning Environment on the Academic Achievement of at Risk Students. In H.C. Waxman and C.D. Ellette (Eds.) *The Study of Learning Environments*, 5, 92-100. College of Education, University of Houston.

Willms, J. and Cohen, M. (1989). The Effects of Ability Grouping on the Ethnic Achievement Gap in Israeli Elementary Schools. *American Journal of Education*, 97(3), 237-257.

Willms, J.D. (1992). Monitoring School Performance : A Guide for Educators, London : The Palmer Press.

Index

L

M

N

O

P

W